THE CHICKEN FARM
AND OTHER SACRED PLACES

| DISCIPLESHIP
ESSENTIALS

A Beautiful Way
An Invitation to a Jesus-Centered Life
by Dan Baumann

The Leadership Paradox
A Challenge to Servant Leadership in a Power-Hungry World
by Denny Gunderson

Learning to Love People You Don't Like
by Floyd McClung

The Chicken Farm and Other Sacred Places
The Joy of Serving God in the Ordinary
by Ken Barnes

DISCIPLESHIP
ESSENTIALS

THE CHICKEN FARM
AND OTHER SACRED PLACES

The Joy of Serving God in the Ordinary

Ken Barnes

YWAM PUBLISHING
Seattle, Washington

YWAM Publishing is the publishing ministry of Youth With A Mission. Youth With A Mission (YWAM) is an international missionary organization of Christians from many denominations dedicated to presenting Jesus Christ to this generation. To this end, YWAM has focused its efforts in three main areas: (1) training and equipping believers for their part in fulfilling the Great Commission (Matthew 28:19), (2) personal evangelism, and (3) mercy ministry (medical and relief work).

For a free catalog of books and materials, call (425) 771-1153 or (800) 922-2143. Visit us online at www.ywampublishing.com

The Chicken Farm and Other Sacred Places: The Joy of Serving God in the Ordinary
Copyright © 2011 by Ken Barnes

Published by YWAM Publishing
a ministry of Youth With A Mission
P.O. Box 55787, Seattle, WA 98155

First printing 2011

Library of Congress Cataloging-in-Publication Data
Barnes, Ken.
    The chicken farm and other sacred places : the joy of serving God in the ordinary / Ken Barnes.
        p. cm.
    Includes bibliographical references (p.   ).
    ISBN 978-1-57658-553-5
    1. Service (Theology) 2. Christian youth—Religious life. 3. Barnes, Ken. 4. Youth with a Mission, Inc. I. Title.
    BV4531.3.B36 2011
    266'.023730092—dc22
    [B]   2010042231

Unless otherwise noted, Scripture quotations are taken from the NEW AMERICAN STANDARD BIBLE®, Copyright © 1960, 1962, 1963, 1968, 1971, 1972, 1973, 1975, 1977, 1995 by The Lockman Foundation. Used by permission.

Printed in the United States of America

To all the unnoticed, unheralded, yet faithful servants of God who have worked down through the years with Youth With A Mission.

And to my wife Sharon, my daughters Deborah and Kendra, my grandson Noah, and all my descendants who might follow. I leave this book with you as a remembrance of my life and, more importantly, as a remembrance of the God that I serve.

↻ Contents

↺ Preface

It was a beautiful July morning in 2007 as I strolled along the beach in North Myrtle Beach, South Carolina. I was struggling because I questioned whether I was qualified to write this book. Being sort of ordinary, did I really have anything to say? A few weeks earlier I had written the first few sentences of this book. People in my church had been encouraging me to put into print some of the stories I had told in my discipleship classes. I was ambivalent. I did have a desire to write a book, but then everybody and their uncle wants to write a book. I wasn't interested in writing a book just to say I had written a book.

One night in early June, God intervened. I found myself wide awake at about 3:00 AM. Normally when I am awakened at this hour, God is prodding me to pray for someone. No one came to my mind. Then an unexpected thought entered my mind, *Why don't you start on your book?* I took a pad and a pencil and that was the beginning of the project.

Back at the beach that morning, as I walked along I cried out to God and told him that I did not know how to write a book. The names of prominent Christian authors crossed my mind, and a series of doubts invaded my thinking. *Who do you think you are? You think you can write a book? Do you really think anybody will want to read your book? Nobody is going to read your book.* What little enthusiasm and passion I had for my writing project started to dissipate like air from a punctured balloon.

I felt small enough to walk right under the crest of the waves crashing on the shore.

But then a still small voice started to speak to my mind and heart. It challenged the validity of all my negative impressions. I remember the words of that gentle voice as if it happened yesterday: "It doesn't matter, as long as I do it for God. If many read the book, or if nobody reads it, it doesn't matter, as long as I have done it for him!" I wanted to laugh, I wanted to cry. Over and over I said to myself, "It doesn't matter, it doesn't matter, as long as I do it for him."

That morning I started to understand that the average nature of my Christian experience did not disqualify me but actually qualified me to write this book. This book is not about the strong and the mighty but about the imperfect yet faithful servants of God in this world. I might not have a lot to say about me, but I have a whole bunch to say about God.

I also realized that morning that my motivation for writing this book needed to be an extension of the book's central message: to encourage people to live for God and his glory. Not for what I could get, but for what I could give. I decided to write the book as a love letter to God and to affirm all of his little ones whom he has called to the high position of serving. If God chooses to share his love letter with many, that is fine. If he chooses to keep it to himself, that is okay also. It is not about me, but about him.

So here it is, Lord—this one is for you. Do with it as you please!

↻ Acknowledgments

I am hesitant to write this section because one knows that it is virtually impossible to mention all who have influenced a life. But let me recognize a few.

At the top of the list is my family. First, I would like to thank my wife, Sharon, who became a book widow for more than a year to facilitate its writing. Her critiques were such a valued part of this project. My daughters, Deborah and Kendra, took on the first editing roles. They, unlike their dad, knew what verb agreement meant. Thank you. I would like to thank my mom, who is ninety-four years young and who took me to Sunday school, where I first learned about God.

I could not have completed this work had it not been for the love, support, and encouragement of a local body of believers, Messiah Christian Church. To people like Betty Dunivan, whose English teaching skills helped correct much of the bad grammar, and Linda Gardner, who gently but consistently (when I procrastinated) never let me forget that I had promised to put the stories I had told at church into print—thank you.

Additionally, I would like to express my gratitude to Carlon Robinson, one of my colleagues at Douglas S. Freeman High School, for her encouragement. She never quit saying to me, "Ken, this thing is going to happen."

I would be remiss if I did not recognize all the YWAMers I worked with for seventeen years and the roles that they took in shaping these stories. I am deeply indebted to those

11

YWAM leaders and followers with whom I labored, for both were shining examples of God's servant heart. I must mention two in particular: Dave Gustaveson, my friend and mentor, who taught me how to write in a way that people enjoy reading; and Nick Savoca, my big brother in the Lord, who from the first time he reviewed my manuscript, championed my cause and worked to get this book published. When my faith wavered, his never did. Thank you.

Last, but in no way least, I want to thank the Lord Jesus, who came not to be served but to serve.

🔃 Introduction

Do you feel ordinary? Do you feel too inadequate, too unqualified, or too overlooked to do great things? Are you unsure of why God put you on this earth? If so, this book is for you. It is for ordinary people who serve an extraordinary God, whose eyes are not only on the red and blue birds in life but also on the plain brown sparrows of this world. Man looks at the outward appearance, but God looks at the heart (1 Sam. 16:7). He takes note of every act of service done in love, and he never, ever forgets such acts.

This is not a how-to book; it does not major on *how* to serve. Rather, it addresses *why* we serve. This is a book about how God works in mysterious ways. It illustrates how God can use the ordinary and even mundane experiences of our lives to teach us about himself in ways we could never learn in a classroom. It shows how holy places—such as a chicken farm, a kitchen, and a steel mill—can affect that critical eighteen inches between head knowledge and heart knowledge. The stories you will read are lessons about how God desperately wants to instill in all of us a servant's heart. "For even the Son of Man did not come to be served, but to serve, and give His life a ransom for many" (Mark 10:45).

This book highlights a hidden group of people who live in various locations and do many different things and yet have similar feelings of being overlooked, underrecognized, and unnoticed. It is about soldiers of faith who are willing to be unknown so that the God they serve can be known. It is about "unnotables" working behind the scenes, laying down their lives for the notables of this world. It is about the unsung heroes of this world who A. W. Tozer once described as "unsung but singing: this is a short and simple story of many today whose names are not know beyond the small circle of their own company. Their gifts are not many nor great, but their song is sweet and clear!"[1]

This book is also about a God who takes notice of the unnotables, who recognizes those whom the world considers to be the least recognizable. This God specializes in taking a little and making it much when his servants are willing to stand up and be known for who they really are, in their strengths and their weaknesses.

This book also describes some of my own journey. It is an incomplete journey, an unfinished story about how God has worked to develop a servant's heart in me. No one ever arrives. God's work in our lives is always ongoing. So come and see what God can do in the most unexpected places and with the least likely people.

Part 1

The Chicken Farm

↺ Chapter 1

From Frostbite to Paradise

When the door of the aircraft swung open, the warm and fragrant aromas of plumeria and other tropical flowers wafted up my nose. Talk about aromatherapy!

When I stepped outside of my classroom, the air was so cold it took my breath away. I thought I was going to freeze to death. The bitter cold western Pennsylvania winter of 1977 took its toll on the public schools where I worked as a teacher. My wife Sharon, my daughter Deborah, and I lived in a small mining community. The subfreezing temperatures produced fuel shortages and long lines at gas stations. Yellow buses stood empty and parked, for lack of fuel. Our bus ramp no longer had the smell of diesel exhaust. School officials in need of solutions scratched their heads in frustration. Schools were forced to close. The students were delighted, of course.

Four years earlier, on my college campus, I had an experience that changed my life. Growing up, I knew about God and had heard all the stories in church. But I hadn't conceived that I could know God personally. I only knew cold and dutiful religion. I was awarded all the Sunday school attendance pins, but what did it matter? I couldn't earn my way into heaven.

A group of students from my alma mater, California State College (now California University of Pennsylvania), attended Urbana 73, a huge student-orientated evangelism and missions conference. Inspired by their experience, the group decided to put on a small version of Urbana on our own campus. One of the students attended my church and invited me to the meetings. A man named Loren Cunningham had traveled all the way from Switzerland to speak. I had never heard of Mr. Cunningham, but I figured if he had come all the way from Switzerland, he must have something important to say. So I decided to go.

I don't remember much of what Loren Cunningham said that night. But one of his points did strike a chord with me. He said, "God does not want half of you; God does not want three-quarters of you; God wants *all* of you." I remember thinking, *This must be my problem!* When Loren gave an invitation, I felt an urge to go forward and make a total commitment to Christ. But there was one problem. Sitting on the gym bleachers in front of me was one of my church elders. I wrestled with my thoughts. *If I go forward, my elder will think I have been a hypocrite!* (Which, of course, I was. But I didn't want him to know it.) Somehow I mustered enough courage to stand up. I walked down the bleacher aisle, focusing my eyes away from the elder, and moved toward the platform. I don't remember exactly what I prayed, but it went something like this: "God, you are not getting much, but whatever there is, you can have all of it." This was the start of my journey of faith.

Four years later, back in the frozen wasteland of the winter of 1977, I sensed that God had something for me to do, but I had no clue what it was. A flyer arrived, advertising a leadership training school run by an organization called Youth With A Mission (YWAM). I found out later that the founder of this organization was none other than Loren Cunningham. I didn't remember Loren saying anything about YWAM at my college that night, but God has a way of filling in the blanks. He takes seemingly disjointed segments of our lives and puts them together like a cosmic jigsaw puzzle to accomplish his will and purpose in our lives.

I was awarded all the Sunday school attendance pins, but what did it matter? I couldn't earn my way into heaven.

The first piece of my jigsaw puzzle was to be, of all places, the South Seas paradise of Hawaii. As my days in Pennsylvania wore on, an urgency to attend this leadership training school grew in my heart. But this created a new hurdle. The school was located in Kona, Hawaii, and I was a poor thirty-year-old schoolteacher from Pennsylvania who had never even been on an airplane! To further complicate things, I would have to convince a number of people—in particular the elders of my church, who oversaw the finances for supporting people like me—that in the midst of one of the harshest winters in decades, I was called by God to Hawaii for a conference. The whole idea seemed crazy. But the more I prayed, the more the idea consumed me.

So now the tough job: persuading the elders, with icicles hanging from my nose, that I was called to this Polynesian paradise. With sweaty palms and an elevated heart rate, I approached my church leaders. Amazingly, their response was positive, and they said a check would be coming in a couple of weeks. The check arrived, and it was not just any check. It was drawn out of the Bank of Heaven. Even now, thirty years later, I still remember the exact amount: $585.00. When I phoned the travel agent to price my plane ticket, the agent responded, "$585.00." I couldn't believe my ears. I guess God knew the confirmation I needed in my first experience in stepping out in faith.

Images of Hawaii danced in my head as I excitedly made preparations to leave for the Aloha State. On a cold February morning I arrived at the Pittsburgh International Airport and boarded my United Airlines flight to Chicago. From there I caught a nonstop flight to Honolulu. My trip culminated with a connection to the Big Island. It felt unreal: in the middle of winter I would be spending twenty-five days in paradise, feasting on God's Word. Little did I know what God had in store for me in this place.

⟐ Chapter 2

Poultry in Paradise

"Lord, do you know that chickens are pretty stupid animals? You do, huh? I assume that, being God, you also know I don't like getting dirt under my fingernails!"

I had arrived at this crossroads of the Pacific with one agenda—to attend a training school and then return home to Pennsylvania—but God had another one. Toward the end of the school, God spoke to me out of Jeremiah 42:10, which begins, "If you will indeed stay in this land . . ." Was I to stay in Hawaii? After a month-long leave of absence from my teaching position, I would now have to resign. This would be quite a leap of faith. My dad and some of Sharon's family were not very excited about this decision, to say the least. My dad was a good man and was sincerely concerned for his son. One day he got his times mixed up and called Hawaii in the middle of the night. "What if things don't work out for you way over there in Hawaii? Are you sure you want to do this?" he asked. I was sure.

And so Sharon and our eighteen-month-old daughter, Deborah, flew to Hawaii. We were together in paradise. Debbie, with her big blue eyes and shining blonde hair, looked like an angel sent from heaven as she walked with us on the sea wall with the aqua blue Pacific Ocean as a backdrop. Sharon and I attended a three-month Discipleship Training School, the beginning course for all prospective YWAM missionaries. Our time was split between schooling and helping out around the training center.

I Have a Problem!

When we finished our training school, Sharon and I felt directed by the Lord to return to western Pennsylvania to put things in order to come back to Hawaii. After an extended stay in the Keystone State, we traveled to the YWAM center in New Hampshire as a preparatory step to return to Hawaii. I worked on what we called a "Truth Penetration Team." We secured jobs in the community to share the gospel with our fellow workers and to save money to pay for our training courses. I worked in a match factory. As we used to say, "You can really get on fire for your job."

During my breaks at the match factory, I felt impressed by the Lord to do a character study on the life of Moses. Sitting on the top of ink cans in my work area, I studied the life of this man. I learned many things about Moses, but one central theme rose above all the others, what I call *kingdom-mindedness*. Let me explain.

In Numbers 14 the people were grumbling and complaining, threatening to appoint another leader and return to Egypt. They were saying things to Moses that most of us have never said (I kid). It seems that the Lord had had enough when he said to Moses, "How long will this people spurn Me? And how long will they not believe in Me, despite all the signs which I have performed in their midst? I will smite them with pestilence and dispossess them, and I will make you into a nation greater and mightier than they" (vv. 11, 12).

What an offer! With Moses, God was going to start over again, and this time without all those complaining and grumbling people. The new nation would be better than the former one. I often wonder how I would have responded if God had made this offer to me. Moses could have had it all, but he responded humbly. "Pardon, I pray, the iniquity of this people according to the greatness of Your lovingkindness, just as You also have forgiven this people, from Egypt even until now" (v. 19). And God graciously pardoned them according to Moses's request.

I was inspired by the life and character of Moses because he exhibited this kingdom-mindedness. Kingdom-mindedness is the attitude of the heart and mind where one is more concerned about the good of the kingdom than one's own good or the good of one's ministry. To put it simply, a kingdom-minded person is an unselfish person. I came to the conclusion that most of Moses's character traits were developed over time and not just inborn or bestowed quickly. They were learned during Moses's forty years on the backside of nowhere, serving his father-in-law and his herds.

When I finished my study, I realized I had a problem. I was not like Moses. Honestly, I was not even remotely kingdom-minded. Selfish was a better description of my character. And so I prayed, "Lord, make me like this man." Be careful of the prayers that you pray, especially the short ones, because God never forgets.

A Chicken Farm?

After our family returned to Hawaii in the spring of 1979, Sharon and I were blessed with the birth of our second daughter, Kendra. She was a beautiful baby. She took after her mother, of course.

In 1979 I attended a YWAM school for people who had a heart to serve the church. After this school, I felt ready to take on the world. A desire to see new evangelism and missions programs released into the body of Christ pulsated in my heart. Raring to go, I sought God's direction. I prayed, but the heavens were like brass. Had God gone off duty?

The days stretched into weeks, and
the effect of isolation took its toll.
My attitude started to change.

I needed something to do temporarily until I had clarity about my next step, so I decided to visit the personnel office. The woman in personnel said to me with a slight smile, "We do have one pressing need. We need people to work on our chicken farm."

"A chicken farm?"

A wealthy chicken farmer from California had offered to give YWAM all we needed to start producing eggs if we would provide the labor to build the farm. And here I was, a former schoolteacher who didn't like to get dirt under my fingernails. The whole idea seemed like a bad dream. There was one other job option, but believe it or not, it was even less enticing than chicken farming. That option was working on the training center's sewage system. A missionary honey-dipper would have been an apt description. So being the spiritual giant that I was, I agreed (somewhat grudgingly) to help out on the farm.

The chicken farm was located on a spot of land *mauka* (Hawaiian for "toward the mountain"), several miles from the main training facility. It was a beautiful but isolated location. A supervisor, several other workers, and I reported for work the first day. There we were, with the trees and the geckos and that was about it. We undertook the task of building the structures to house the chickens, mostly from solid Hawaiian lava rock.

The days stretched into weeks, and the effect of isolation took its toll. Gone were the familiar sounds of the training center's activities. My attitude started to change. Work was not exciting. Instead of "Good morning, Lord," it was more like "Good Lord, it's morning." Occasionally, a leader visited the building site and walked past me like I didn't exist (or at least I imagined they didn't notice me). Have you ever felt like you have fallen off the face of the earth and no one is looking for you? Returning from work one day, I said to my wife, "Pinch me and see if I'm real. Maybe I'm just a mirage."

To make matters worse, I had an identity crisis. Sharon had become my alter ego. She served as the base nurse, worked in the counseling ministry, and knew just about everybody— sort of the life of the party. Meeting new people at the center took on an interesting twist for me. "Hello, my name is Ken Barnes." "Oh yeah, you're Sharon Barnes's husband." I would think to myself, *Yeah, that's me, Sharon Barnes's husband.*

Things started coming out of my mouth which were at best somewhat negative and at worst outright grumbling. Little comments to my supervisor let him know that I was not a happy camper. I never came right out and said it, since that would have been too obvious and unspiritual. I was losing my joy.

Things continued in this downward spiral until one day I decided that I was going to have it out with God. Little did I know that an encounter with the Almighty would change the entire course of my life.

That morning I had had enough. When I opened the door of the brooder house, the pungent odor of chicken manure pushed me over the edge. I threw my rake on the floor and complained, "I am tired of working on this chicken farm! I did not come here to work on a farm and clean up after stupid chickens!" In the midst of my tirade, I said something that must have really caught God's attention: "Nobody cares whether I work up here. No one even sees me."

Have you ever felt like you have
fallen off the face of the earth and
no one is looking for you?

Immediately, God dropped a couple of questions into my mind. First: *Why did you come to Hawaii?* Without delay I answered, "Because I wanted to serve you, Lord." The next question penetrated the recesses of my heart: *Don't I see?* I was dumbfounded as the blinders fell from my eyes. Suddenly I saw myself as I really was—I didn't serve God like I thought I did.

When I wasn't noticed, when my purposes were not being fulfilled, when I wasn't doing what I wanted to do, then I did not serve God with joy and gladness. Though I said that I served him, I saw for the first time that morning that so much of my service was based on rewards and recognition from man. I had to honestly admit that I had "I" problems. I served myself more than God.

When God shows us a bit of our hearts, we have a choice to make. We can justify our actions by saying everybody is like this and it is no big deal, or we can repent. I chose to repent. "Forgive me, Lord," I prayed, "and help me to serve you and you alone."

Although I had prayed the prayer, sometimes words are cheap. God had started to work in my heart. He was in the process of changing my understanding of him from head knowledge to heart revelation, from an intellectual understanding of his Word to the application of it in my life. Our hearts don't change quickly, or at least mine didn't. I needed to walk out this newfound truth. I needed to take practical steps to direct my affections and devotion toward him and to place my security in him and him alone.

What did walking it out look like? Right then it looked like picking up the rake I had thrown to the floor in disgust and entering the brooder house. Lifting my rake to heaven, I said, "I'm going to do this for you, today." Then I added, "Lord, when I start to struggle"—and I did—"and when I crave recognition from people, I am going to look to you for recognition and acceptance."

And you know what? From then on, when I did that, God was always there. Was there a dramatic and immediate change in my life? No; I had good days and not-so-good days. But I noticed one difference: my joy started to return. It was two steps forward and one step back, but I was moving in the right direction.

ↄ *Chapter 3*

"Eggucation": Lessons from the Chicken Farm

"There goes another plane leaving the Kona airport loaded with missionaries, and I am not on it. I'm still stuck here on this farm with these chickens."

P rior to, during, and for some time after the chicken-farm experience, I was really clueless about why God led me the way he did. Glimpses of understanding would come into focus, but the big picture still was off the radar screen. And yet the setting God chose should have been a dead giveaway (more on that below).

A biblical scene continued to come to my mind. The scene is from John 13, where Jesus is washing the disciples' feet. I was particularly drawn to verse 7, where Jesus talks to Peter. Jesus says, "What I do you do not realize now, but you will understand hereafter." As I look back on my experience, I see that God was trying to teach me something about serving that I would not understand till later. What was it about serving that God wanted me to know?

The Vertical Principle

The initial step in acquiring a servant's heart is learning to serve God first. Anything that competes with our affections for God will impede our serving him. Galatians 1:10 says, "For am I now seeking the favor of men, or of God? Or am I striving to please men? If I were still trying to please men, I would not be a bond-servant of Christ." Up to this point I was a man-pleaser, and that had to die before I could truly serve God.

The chicken farm overlooked the Kona International Airport. The bright runways were a stark contrast to the dark lava flows of the Big Island. I watched planes take off, some carrying our ministry teams going to Hong Kong, Thailand, the Pacific Islands, and various other locations in Asia. I often thought to myself, *If I could just get on one of those planes and get out to Asia and evangelize. I could get a few notches on my Bible, and then I would really be somebody.* I wanted to be on one of those planes so badly I could taste it. I wanted to have some real missionary stories to send to my church's missions committee, instead of those somewhat embarrassing letters about working on a chicken farm.

In retrospect, I think God was saying, "Ken, if you are not a somebody on this farm, then you are never going to be a somebody out in Asia. Because you are not a somebody based on what you can do, but who you are in me." I could know my true value only if I knew what God and God alone thought about me.

God was dealing with a heart issue. He was reorienting the inclination of my heart so that my security would be in him and my praise would be from him. Romans 2:29 says, "But he is a Jew who is one inwardly; and circumcision is that which is of the heart, by the Spirit, not by the letter; and *his praise is not from men, but from God*" (emphasis added). God was doing radical heart surgery, a circumcision of my heart, so that it would be inclined first toward God and not man. The scripture indicates that this happens by the Spirit, not by the letter of the law. I cannot change my heart—this is a sovereign work of grace. But I can obey him by inclining my heart toward truth. This is not a story about willpower; it's about God's will, my obedience, and God's power. Obedience means that we keep ourselves in the place that God has provided as he works in our lives. And that we can do.

I could know my true value only
if I knew what God and God
alone thought about me.

We were often told in our training, "You do the possible, and God will do the impossible." And God surely did the impossible (changing my heart) as I did the possible (obeying him). Not that it was a finished process, but the process began in that holy place called the chicken farm.

The setting of God's dealings with me should have sent an obvious message. In *Celebration of Discipline,* Richard Foster refers to how the discipline of service frees us from worldly games of promotion and authority. "It abolishes our need (and desire) for a 'pecking order.'" He goes on to illustrate how people are a lot like chickens. "In the chicken pen there is no peace until it is clear who is the greatest and who is the least and who is at which rung everywhere in between."[2] God was giving me a little show-and-tell to teach me the foolishness of comparing myself with others.

Through this experience, I arrived at two conclusions. First, how creatively detailed and humorous God can be in revealing himself to us. And second, how clueless his sheep are sometimes. Can you imagine a conversation among the Trinity? "Can we make it any clearer to him? I guess we could have written it on the wall."

The God of the Ordinary

Someone once said, "The problem with the Christian life is that it is every day." My farming experience illustrates how God can use ordinary people (or chickens) and ordinary situations to teach us extraordinary lessons. Yet we can miss these lessons just because they are in such mundane settings.

Alistair Begg, senior pastor of Parkside Church in Cleveland, Ohio, preached a message called "The God of the Ordinary," in which he expounded on how most of our lives are ordinary and rather humdrum.[3] He alluded to the fact that most of us, if we are honest, feel insignificant in the grand scheme of things. Pastor Begg argued that most of us wrongly believe that "ordinariness is the precursor to uselessness," which is why we "go in search of the unusual and the spectacular." We seek the mountaintop experience just beyond the horizon. We develop a bad case of what I call "horizonitis," fixing our gaze entirely on the spectacular spiritual event beyond the rainbow, and missing the little opportunities for service and the spiritual blessing which God has placed right in front of us. The truth of the matter, Pastor Begg states, is that God does not need us to be unusual or spectacular.

Have you ever wondered what it might feel like to be a sparrow living in a world full of red and blue birds? Maybe you haven't, but I think many people already know. Who am I in relation to the grand and cosmic plans and purposes of the Creator of the universe? How could the God who flung the billions upon billions of stars into existence and holds everything in place by his watchful eye have time to turn his eye just toward me? Have you ever felt this way?

The sparrow is small with little distinguishing characteristics. We hear all the time, "Look at the beautiful red bird," or blue bird, or majestic eagle. Yet the Bible says not even a sparrow, worth only a half penny, "can fall to the ground without your Father knowing it" (Matt. 10:29 NLT). Jesus chose to use this seemingly small and insignificant bird as an example of the Father's care and watchful eye. Take to heart, my friends, the words of a song that has become famous in American churches, "His Eye Is on the Sparrow":

> Why should I feel discouraged, why should the shad-
> ows come,
> Why should my heart be lonely, and long for heaven
> and home,
> When Jesus is my portion? My constant friend is He:
> His eye is on the sparrow, and I know He watches me.

If God is watching, that is enough.

When the first egg we produced rolled into the basket, I felt a sense of satisfaction and accomplishment. Peace filled my heart. I had learned to be content to provide food so others could go to Asia and preach the gospel. Their success became my success. Serving God was not a competition but a partnership, and I played a small but no less significant part in that process. If only God and I realized this, that was enough.

The Keeper of the Spring

Dr. Peter Marshall, the famous preacher and chaplain of the US Senate, loved to tell the following story.

> The Keeper of the Spring, was a quiet forest dweller who lived high above an Austrian village along the eastern slopes of the Alps. The old gentleman had been hired many years ago by a young town council to clear away the debris from the pools of water up in the mountain crevices that fed the lovely spring flowing through their town. With faithful, silent,

regularity he patrolled the hills, removed the leaves and branches, and wiped away the silt that would otherwise contaminate the fresh flow of water. By and by, the village became a popular attraction for vacationers. Graceful swans floated along the crystal clear spring, the millwheels of various businesses located near the water turned day and night, farmlands were naturally irrigated, and the view from restaurants was picturesque beyond description.

Years passed. One evening the town council met for its semiannual meeting. As they reviewed the budget, one man's eye caught the salary figure of the obscure keeper of the spring. Said the keeper of the purse, "Who is the old man? Why do we keep him on year after year? No one ever sees him. For all we know that strange ranger of the hills is doing no good. He isn't necessary any longer." By a unanimous vote, they dispensed with the old man's services.

For several weeks nothing changed. By early autumn the trees started to shed their leaves. Small branches snapped off and fell into the pools, hindering the rushing flow of sparkling water. One afternoon someone noticed a slight yellowish-brown tint in the spring. A couple of days later the water was much darker. Within another week, a slimy film covered sections of the water along the banks and a foul odor was soon detected. The millwheels moved slower and then some ground to a halt. Swans left as well as the tourists. Clammy fingers of disease and sickness reached deeply into the village.

Quickly, the embarrassed council called a special meeting. Realizing their gross error in judgment, they hired back the keeper of the spring . . . and within a few weeks the veritable river of life began to clear up. The wheels started to turn, and new life returned to the hamlet in the Alps once again.[4]

Chuck Swindoll comments about this story: "What the 'Keeper of the Spring' meant to the village, Christian servants mean to our world. The preserving, taste-giving bite of salt and the illuminating, hope-giving ray of light may seem feeble and needless . . . but God help any society that attempts to exist without them."[5]

I would add, God help any church or mission that attempts this, too. This story is a fitting tribute to those of this world who have the high calling of service to God.

U Chapter 4

An Attitude of Gratitude

The sound of the swats from the hickory stick reverberated in the ears of the students. How long is this going to take? *they wondered.*

Prior to coming to Hawaii, my wife and I had good jobs, and finances were never a major concern for us. Our financial situation changed when we joined YWAM: all volunteers had to raise their own financial support. In the early years of our experience in missions, things were pretty tight financially. We had to budget our support carefully and keep our nonessential spending to a bare minimum. We allowed ourselves to have a treat once a week. The treat would be a bag of potato chips to go with our weekend lunch sandwiches. Or sometimes we would get really daring and buy a half gallon of ice cream. We were definitely not living high on the hog.

On a normal Saturday morning, you would find me going to a little village about a mile from our training center to purchase our chips for lunch. We had no car, so I walked. One time, as I made my trek to the village store, my attitude wasn't what it should have been. I was becoming resentful that I didn't have a car and had to walk up and down the highway when we needed something. On many of these Saturday mornings I would see a guy drive past in his new Mercedes Benz. *Maybe he's going to the local racquet club. He probably doesn't care at all about God,* I would think to myself. On this morning when he drove past me, it appeared he double-clutched (though I could very well have imagined it), and diesel exhaust blew in my face. It was like adding insult to injury. Then, in line at the village store I noticed people placing all kinds of expensive desserts on the checkout belt, and there I was with my toothpaste and chips. We don't care how much other people have as long as it is not more than us.

Sometime later, on a bright morning in the midst of my weekly journey along the highway, God interrupted my little pity party. As I was pondering all that I didn't have, in a still small voice God said to me, "Give me thanks." My response showed the condition of my heart. "For what?" I said. Then I looked down at my feet and saw my flip-flops (no one wears shoes in Hawaii), and the thought occurred to me, *I can thank him for these, because many people in the world have no shoes to wear.* Walking down that road, I thanked God for my footwear. Then I expressed my appreciation for having the health and strength to walk to the store. Many people in the world would give all they owned to be able to take one walk to the store.

My human nature by itself always seems to dwell on what I don't have rather than what I do have. When I simply recognize God's blessings and am grateful for what God has given me, my whole attitude starts to change. The enemy of our souls thrives on ungratefulness and discontent, and we give him the ammunition to fire at us by choosing to dwell on what we lack rather than on God's blessings. The antidotes for self-pity are gratefulness and contentment. "Now godliness with contentment is great gain" (1 Tim. 6:6 NKJV). In the final analysis, gratefulness is an attitude of heart and is based not on our circumstances but on God's goodness. Walking along that road in Kona, I learned how gratefulness and contentment allowed my eyes to be opened to the goodness of God.

Ultimately, gratefulness emanates from what God has done for us through his Son, Jesus Christ.

A Kentucky Rose

Why do we do what we do? Why do we serve God? The motive behind our actions is critically important to our spiritual development. God is not only concerned with how we serve him but why we serve him. This is made clear in Matthew 20:25–28:

> But Jesus called them to Himself and said, "You know that the rulers of the Gentiles lord it over them, and their great men exercise authority over them.
>
> "It is not this way among you, but whoever wishes to become great among you shall be your servant, and whoever wishes to be first among you shall be your slave; just as the Son of Man did not come to be served, but to serve, and to give His life a ransom for many."

In verse 26 the word "servant" in Greek is *diakonos*: one who ran errands, waited tables, and did menial tasks. In verse 27 the word "slave" is *doulos*: a bondservant. This was a person who could have had his freedom but chose to serve his master, not out of compulsion, but out of love. If you want to be great, then serve. If you want to be first among those who serve, do it not just because you feel you must, but out of a motivation of love. First John 4:19 says, "We love Him because He first loved us" (NKJV). Before we did one act of service, before we committed one act of selfless sacrifice, Jesus loved us. Our commitment to him is not to win his love—we already have it. It is in response to this great love that we follow him. The following story illustrates this type of self-giving love.

Nestled in the hills of Kentucky sat a little one-room school house. The kids in this school were a pretty rough bunch. Some boys were already shaving in the second grade. The school was without a teacher because the students had run off every teacher that came their way.

We don't care how much other people have as long as it is not more than us.

A little man arrived in town one day who had teaching credentials. He learned of the job opening and inquired of the chairman of the school board about the position. The chairman asked, "Have you heard what happened to all our other teachers?" The man nodded that he had and said he would still like the job. So the chairman thought, *What do I have to lose?* and he hired the man.

Word was sent throughout the community that school would resume the following week. Monday morning the students arrived with spitballs in their pockets, prepared to commence the onslaught. They sized up the diminutive stature of the teacher and smirked. This was going to be even easier than the others! But before they could get the spitballs out of their pockets, the teacher made a statement that took the students by surprise. "Since you are going to have to follow the rules in this school," he said, "you should have a part in deciding what the rules should be." The kids thought to themselves, *This is different,* and left their spitballs in their pockets, waiting to hear what the teacher would say next.

The teacher asked, "What rules do you think we should have?" A studious-looking girl with horn-rimmed glasses said, "I think it should be wrong to cheat off of other students' papers." The teacher said, "That's a good rule," and he wrote it down. Next, a little chubby boy in the second row stood up and said, "I think it should be wrong to steal lunches." No doubt, the other kids had made a habit of taking his lunch. The teacher agreed that this was a good classroom rule and recorded it. A tiny boy in the back of the room who looked like he was picked on all the time sheepishly put up his hand and said, "I think it should be wrong to hit people with spitballs." The teacher nodded and wrote it down. This went on until the teacher and the students felt they had enough rules to run the classroom.

The teacher said, "A rule without a consequence is not a rule; it is just advice." So the kids, along with the teacher, assigned a punishment for each infraction. The method of punishment in this school was swats with a hickory stick.

Class began, and to everyone's amazement, except maybe the teacher's, no one broke a rule. This continued until one day the little chubby boy, looking extremely hungry, approached the teacher and said, "Someone stole my lunch." The teacher quickly summoned the class to their seats.

"Someone has stolen a lunch," he said. The class was indignant. How dare someone break one of the rules!

One of the students shouted out, "This person must come forward and be punished!"

"Who stole the lunch?" the teacher said sternly. No one said a word. The teacher asked again, "Who took the lunch?" Again, there was total silence. A third time, with a raised voice, he said, "Who stole the lunch?"

After a short delay, a small boy named Johnny got up from the back of the room and walked forward. Johnny came from one of the poorest families in the community. This was evident from his attire. It was the middle of winter, and he was dressed in jeans, an outer jacket but no shirt, and shoes but no socks.

The teacher looked puzzled—stealing was totally out of character for Johnny. He looked at Johnny and said, "Why did you do it? Why did you steal the lunch?"

Johnny replied, "There hasn't been much money at home lately, and I hadn't eaten for three days. I was hungry and I took his lunch." The teacher swallowed, wondering what he should do. If he did not administer the punishment, would all the rest of the rules be ignored? On the other hand, how could he punish a boy who had not eaten for three days? Hesitantly, the teacher arrived at his decision: the consequence must be administered.

The teacher slowly moved toward the cupboard and got the hickory stick. As he was walking back, stick in hand, an older boy in the class named Jim asked, "Teacher, is there any rule that says someone can't take someone else's punishment?"

The teacher thought for a moment and said, "No, there is no rule against that. But the consequence must be administered." A hush fell over the room.

The silence was broken as Jim walked forward and bent over the front desk. The teacher instructed the rest of the class to put their heads down on their desks and close their eyes. The punishment commenced as the sound of the swats rang in the students' ears. It only took a few moments, but to the students it seemed an eternity. Finally the sound stopped, and one by one the students lifted their heads, quickly drying their eyes to hide their tears. In front of the class, Johnny was hugging Jim. As he continued to embrace Jim, the other students fought back more tears. Then Johnny backed away from Jim and looked up into his face and with tears rolling down his little cheeks said, "Jim, even if I have to starve to death, I will never steal another lunch." After that day, wherever Jim would go, Johnny was close behind, never being able to do enough for his newfound friend—the friend who took the punishment that he deserved.

I think you understand the analogy. When we see how Jesus "did not come to be served, but to serve, and to give His life a ransom for many," it revolutionizes our service to him. We will not serve him out of threat, compulsion, or even obligation. We won't *have* to serve; we will *want* to serve. No matter how many sacrifices, no matter how many times we go unnoticed or feel unappreciated, we will remember that we can never outgive God. And like Johnny, we will never be able to do enough for our newfound Friend!

Time to Move On

As time passed, God brought other workers to the farm. My time on the farm came to an end. Sharon and I made plans for our family to go on furlough on the mainland, and upon our return to Hawaii I would move on to a new ministry.

I reflected as I left the farm, "Thank you, Lord. I have learned my lesson, and now I can go out and do what I am supposed to do." Little did I know that the lesson I was learning was multifaceted.

Part 2

The Kitchen and Other Places

U Chapter 5

A Culinary Caper

"Here I am, a thirty-four-year-old gofer, breaking my back carrying produce in a kitchen. This is not my idea of mission work!"

It was 1981. We were about 39,000 feet above the Pacific Ocean in a Boeing 747 returning from furlough. I was gazing out the window with my Bible on my lap, praying and thinking about God's direction for my life. Deep down in my inner being I knew God was going to reveal to me my future direction. I was reading Exodus 17 and was drawn to the part where Moses was leading Israel in battle against the Amalekites. With his staff in his hands, Moses extended his arms above his head, and Israel prevailed in the battle. As Moses's arms became heavy and fell to his side, the battle turned in favor of the enemy. Aaron and Hur quickly rushed to Moses's aid. With Moses seated, each of them supported an arm, and Israel again became victorious.

I felt a rush in my emotions. Was I to be like Aaron and Hur? Was God going to have me come alongside of one of the mission leaders? Several people flashed through my mind; all of them were leaders at the training center. I envisioned myself with several of them in ministry situations. Closing my Bible, my expectancy continued to peak as I pondered who this person would turn out to be.

We arrived in sunny Kona and proceeded to get back into the swing of things. One Saturday I found myself harvesting bananas with our cook, Hans-Rudi. In the course of the morning, Hans-Rudi said, "Ken, we have so much work to do in the kitchen and so few workers. We are really understaffed." My mind drifted back to the plane and to Aaron and Hur holding up Moses's arms. *God, is this the person?* After a momentary pause, I said to myself, *No way,* and dismissed the thought. We finished the harvesting, and I went on my way trying my best to forget this little incident.

A day or two later I received a phone call. Guess who it was on the other end of the line? The woman from personnel, the same woman who had suggested I give chicken farming a try! I knew I was in trouble. You probably already know what she had to say. She mentioned the need in the kitchen and asked if I would help out Hans-Rudi. I told her that I would pray about it, and hung up the phone. I felt as if I had been punched in the stomach. Considering the airplane revelation and the banana-harvesting experience, deep down I already knew what God wanted me to do. But I prayed anyway, hoping God would change his mind. (Sometimes we substitute praying for obeying.) In the end, I called the woman in personnel and agreed to do it: I would try my hand in the kitchen.

What Am I, Limburger Cheese?

I reported to the kitchen. I was thirty-four years old and had become, for lack of a better description, Hans-Rudi's "gofer." If Hans-Rudi needed some carrots, I would go to the cold-storage room (commonly called the cool room) to get them. If he needed potatoes, meat, cheese, or just about anything else, I got it for him. The work did not stimulate my mind a whole lot, but it kept my body really busy. Hans-Rudi had come to us from Switzerland after having worked as a chef at a classy hotel there. He was a great cook. People were always coming by and giving him a hug and congratulating him on the great meals he prepared. As people were hugging Hans-Rudi, I would be lifting a box of vegetables off the kitchen floor. The more they commended him, the more I felt unnoticed. I wanted to say to them, "What am I, Limburger cheese?"

I was showing a telltale sign which surfaces
when God starts to challenge attitudes –
I was once again losing my joy.

Negative thoughts and attitudes started to arise in me. *If I weren't lifting these boxes, Hans-Rudi wouldn't be able to do what he does. But no one seems to notice. This missionary life isn't what it's cracked up to be.* Sounds familiar, doesn't it? I went to work, but not happily. I dwelled on what was wrong with circumstances and people rather than what was right. I became critical, at first mainly in my thought life. Soon little comments, though veiled, spoke volumes about what was going on in my heart. I was showing a telltale sign which surfaces when God starts to challenge attitudes—I was once again losing my joy.

The situation came to a head at a weekly staff meeting. It was the "unsung hero" section of the meeting where we highlighted a staff member's contributions and commitment to the training center. Hans-Rudi was chosen as the unsung hero this night. Remembering all the hugs and congratulations, I sat there thinking, *Hans-Rudi, an unsung hero? Yeah, right!* Hans-Rudi rose to his feet. Person after person stood up and affirmed his culinary skills, his servant heart, and various other things. I on the other hand could not think of one good thing to say—or more correctly, one good thing I *wanted* to say. As a matter of fact, as each person spoke, I became more and more angry. Finally, I couldn't take it any longer, and I got up and left the meeting.

Something was desperately wrong. Why couldn't I stand to hear something good said about a Christian brother? I walked to the field in the back of the meeting area and looked up into the dark of the night. "What is going on, God?" Almost immediately my time in the match factory in New Hampshire and the image of Moses as an unselfish kingdom-builder flashed into my mind's eye. The words to that little prayer invaded my thoughts: "Lord, make me like this man." As clearly as I had ever heard God speak, he said, "Ken, I am just answering your prayer."

I was stunned as God once again confronted me with the condition of my heart. After a few moments, all I could say was, "God, forgive me. Forgive me for the selfishness of my heart."

As I wept before the Lord, he showed me that there needed to be feet to my contrition. My repentance was not just to be words that I said but actions that demonstrated that my words were true. God gave me a plan of action. When I started to complain about where he had placed me, I needed to pray, "Thank you, Lord, for the honor of serving you in this kitchen." When I was tempted to be critical of Hans-Rudi or others I worked with, I needed to call it what it was—envy, jealousy, selfish ambition. Criticism was to be countered with compliments and gratefulness. Can you imagine how the enemy of our soul hates it when we counter his lies with the truth?

I returned to the kitchen with new resolve. And no, everything wasn't a bed of roses from this point forward. The tests came. When criticism and complaining reared their ugly heads, my response was, "Hans-Rudi, you are a great guy"—which he really was—"and I am privileged to work with you." I was not flattering him; I was speaking the truth. As God enabled me to respond in this manner, little by little I started to be victorious over my critical attitude. And you guessed it—my joy started to return. God had done a work in my heart.

My repentance was not just to be words that I said but actions that demonstrated that my words were true.

At the risk of sounding repetitious, let me say again that I did not change my heart; God did. I did what I could do, which was to be obedient. God did the rest. It was God's initiative; it did not start with me or my choices. I responded in obedience, and God's will and power brought it to pass. The process wasn't quick and easy, and it did not happen overnight. But it began as I started to move in the right direction.

On more than one occasion, I bore my emotions before the Lord and said things like, "God, I can't work in this kitchen one more hour." But I was in pretty good company. King David was honest about his difficulties before God. God understands our struggles. He is not taken aback by our weaknesses and frailties. When we make known our feelings of inadequacy, we acknowledge before God that without him we cannot do it. The apostle Paul once said (in 2 Corinthians 12:10), "When I am weak, then I am strong."

Chapter 6

Food for Thought: Lessons from the Kitchen

Clean up after chickens? It's not my bag. Lug around boxes of produce? I have more valuable things to do with my time. I want to live life on the top.

In chapter 3, the first lesson about service was *vertical*: we must learn to serve God and God alone; our affirmation and security must be in him first. My time in the kitchen led me to see a second level or tier that involves a *horizontal* orientation of service. Loving God is the first and most important step, but it is not the only step. Loving man is also part of true service, and this is what I describe as the horizontal principle. It is never just me and Jesus. As we love and serve God, this love must overflow to others.

Gordon MacDonald, in his book *Rebuilding Your Broken World,* says, "You know whether or not you're really a servant by the way you react when you're treated like one."[6] Clearly, I didn't react like a servant in the kitchen. The question is, why did I react as I did? The most obvious reasons are ones I have already mentioned, such as envy, jealousy, and selfish ambition, or what the Bible calls the "deeds of the flesh" (Gal. 5:19). But I think there were deeper and maybe less obvious reasons.

(Not) Free to Serve

Sometimes we confuse position and value. We react to people who may view us as servants because we feel it demeans us. Jesus never reacted this way. Right before he washes his disciples' feet in John 13, it is recorded (v. 3) that "Jesus [knew] that the Father had given all things into His hands, and that He had come forth from God and was going back to God." Jesus had an answer to the three basic philosophical questions of life: Who am I? Where did I come from? And where am I going? As the Son of God, Jesus did not need to derive value from what he did on this earth. He was free to serve. He did not get value from what he did; instead, he brought value to it because of his intrinsic worth as the Son of God.

It is never just me and Jesus.
As we love and serve God, this
love must overflow to others.

Why was I envious and jealous of Hans-Rudi? He had position, and I didn't. Why was rank so important? Because stature represented value to me. Unlike Jesus, I was not free to serve. I did not bring distinction to my work; instead, I sought to get prestige from it. I would serve, but only if I were recognized, because this is what I thought gave me significance. I didn't realize that position pertained only to my function, not my worth.

So what is in it for us? If God is really good and loving, then isn't he always choosing our highest good? How did my experience in the kitchen express his will for my best?

Looking back, I can see that it was God's way of showing me who I was, how I could be truly fulfilled, and how I could be ultimately successful.

Jesus said, "You know that the rulers of the Gentiles lord it over them, and their great men exercise authority over them. It is not this way among you, but whoever wishes to become great among you shall be your servant, and whoever wishes to be first among you shall be your slave; just as the Son of Man did not come to be served, but to serve, and to give His life a ransom for many" (Matt. 20:25–28). The world tells us, if we just get that position, if we just get to the top, then we will be fulfilled and feel good about ourselves. This seems logical, but the problem is that it is logically wrong. How do I know? Ask the people who have gotten there. Ask the people who have risen to the heights in the corporate world or entertainment world or even in religious pursuits. Most of them will tell you that satisfaction in not achieved just by getting to the top. Yes, there is a measure of fulfillment and satisfaction in accomplishments, but only if they are a by-product of our service and desire to glorify God. There is no enduring satisfaction outside of God.

Why do we believe there is fulfillment outside of God? Why do we, if we are honest enough to admit it, crave position, power, and influence, thinking that is what will bring us satisfaction? Some more, some less, but we all have this tendency. I believe the reason we all have this propensity is that we got it from our ancestors, Adam and Eve. When the devil was tempting Eve to eat of the forbidden fruit, he said, "For God knows that in the day you eat from it your eyes will be opened, and you will be like God, knowing good and evil" (Gen. 3:5). Eve was tempted to believe that if she just asserted herself, if she did what she wanted, then she could have what she desired (her fulfillment) outside of and independent of God. *Eve, you don't need God, you can make it happen.* And you know the story: she swallowed the lie and the forbidden fruit, and we have been reaping the consequences of that bite ever since. We pursue fulfillment and success in all the wrong places.

On the chicken farm and in the kitchen, I was reacting according to my nature as a sinful and selfish person. I was doing what came naturally to me. And I think I had (and have) a lot of company in this.

The Power of the Towel

What is it about working on a chicken farm or in a kitchen or countless other places that counteracts this tendency toward self-fulfillment? Let's examine a biblical encounter that sheds some light on this issue.

"You're not washing my feet," Peter protested to the Lord. Jesus, in the last major interaction with his disciples, modeled what to them was a strange and maybe even bizarre act. After he ate his last meal with them, he took a basin of water and wrapped a towel around himself. He then proceeded to perform a task that astounded them. John 13:5 records, "Then He poured water into the basin, and began to wash the disciples' feet and to wipe them with the towel with which he was girded." That night the gates of hell must have rattled as the powers of darkness pondered the revolutionary nature of this act of service. Though not fully birthed, a new mentality was conceived in the hearts of Jesus' followers. This new mindset brought a swift and erroneous reaction from the people of his day. "Here comes the man that is trying to turn the world upside down," people exclaimed. They were partly right: he was trying to turn the world around. But he was not turning it upside down. Instead, he was turning the world right side up. Since the Garden of Eden, the world had been inverted; Jesus was just righting it.

A distinct part of this radical turnaround that Jesus initiated was an others-orientation in our thoughts and actions. In Philippians 2:3–7 the apostle Paul instructs us:

> Do nothing from selfishness or empty conceit, but with humility of mind regard one another as more important than yourselves; do not merely look out for your own personal interests, but also for the interests of others. Have this attitude in yourselves which was also in Christ Jesus, who, although He existed in the form of God, did not regard equality with God a thing to be grasped, but emptied Himself, taking the form of a bond-servant, and being made in the likeness of men.

Jesus, instead of pointing others toward himself, pointed himself toward others. This was the antithesis of the mentality of the world. Even the disciples missed what he was trying to do. In John 13:6–8 Peter (once again) puts his foot in his mouth. "So [Jesus] came to Simon Peter. [Peter] said to Him, 'Lord, do you wash my feet?' Jesus answered and said to him, 'What I do you do not realize now, but you will understand hereafter.' Peter said to Him, 'Never shall You wash my feet!' Jesus answered him, 'If I do not wash you, you have no part with Me.'"

Peter had a pecking-order mentality of value and ministry. Jesus, we wash your feet, and those under us wash our feet, and so on. Jesus blew a hole right in the middle of this mindset as he put himself at the bottom of the pecking-order. The most valuable (Jesus) became the least valuable (the servant), so that all people could know their true value. Then Jesus told his disciples to go and do likewise if they wanted to be great in his kingdom.

On the farm and in the kitchen I was clueless about serving, but I was in pretty good company. Most of the disciples were drawing a blank as they watched the Lord of Glory wash their feet.

God was doing something in their lives, but what was he trying to do *through* their lives? Was Jesus trying to give his disciples and all who would follow a secret weapon, one that would open the hearts of the masses to the gospel? The old saying goes, "People don't care how much you know until they know how much you care." Jesus was leaving with his disciples a tool that would validate their words and penetrate the hearts of those they desired to reach. This was the last night Jesus had with his disciples, the final time before he was glorified to influence their thinking and actions. He forever etched an image on their minds and hearts, the impression of the Son of Man washing feet. He was teaching them the power of the towel.

Chapter 7

The Acid Test

I felt like I was working in the bowels of the earth. Where was God now?

Back in 1977, after Sharon and I returned to Pennsylvania following our first Kona training school, I got a job working in a steel mill just outside Pittsburgh. I worked in an old open-hearth furnace which produced pig iron. I labored in the flues underneath a huge battery of furnaces. It was hot and dirty. It felt as if the soles of my work boots were going to melt. Sometimes it felt like hell to me.

How did I arrive at this place? Several months earlier we had finished our training school in Hawaii. We were sure that God had called us back to western Pennsylvania. I assumed that God was going to open to us a ministry opportunity as we obeyed him and returned to the area where my wife and I both grew up. Things did not go as planned, however, and obedience did not bring the expected new ministry adventure that I had envisioned. I went through a couple of jobs in which I was either marginally successful or not successful at all. In a last-ditch effort to survive financially, I returned to the steel mills where I worked during summer breaks while attending college. This was not supposed to be happening. Had we missed God? We were confused, but it still seemed that God wanted us back in this area for some reason.

The weeks stretched into months, and I drudged through the soot and heat and darkness of the underworld of this steel mill on the banks of the Monongahela River. I pondered the fact that I had given up a good teaching position and was now in what appeared to be a dead-end job. I thought about friends and acquaintances of mine who were involved in teaching or ministry ventures, and I was stuck here in this dungeon with seemingly nothing of any eternal significance happening. Doubt and unbelief began to wrap their filthy little hands around my heart.

I started to feel like I had stepped out for God and he had pulled the rug out from under me. I shrank back into a shell, just trying to survive. No one in my work crew knew I was a believer; I just didn't know if I wanted to stick my neck out for God again. The truth was, I was on the brink of backsliding. I was moving away from the God I had always wanted to serve. I realized that I was coming to a crossroads in relation to my faith. Would I continue to serve the God I had met on my college campus, or had I tried the God thing and it had not worked? Interestingly, God used a little sticker to direct my steps at this intersection of faith and unbelief.

Weeks earlier in a Christian bookstore, a little sticker caught my eye. It simply said, *One Way, Jesus.* I bought the sticker with the intent to put it on the hard safety helmet I wore in the mill. I never placed the sticker on my helmet, but I never lost track of its whereabouts, either. This sort of summed up my condition. I wanted to serve God, but I could not get past the struggles I had faced since returning to

Pennsylvania. A battle raged in my mind between thoughts about the goodness of God as described in the Bible and other mental impressions about the reality of my dismal circumstances. Who would win this battle?

I was coming to a crossroads in relation to my faith. Would I continue to serve the God I had met on my college campus, or had I tried the God thing and it had not worked?

One day I took the sticker out of my dresser drawer and put in my pocket as I left for work. On one of my breaks I went into the bathroom, took the sticker out of my pocket, and gazed at it. The same thoughts pervaded my mind as had been there since I first set foot in that place. One set of thoughts said, *God is good, and he is worthy to be served.* And others screamed, *If God is so good, why has all this happened to you?* The sticker seemed so small and insignificant, but I realized it could have major ramifications for my life. Affixing this little sign to my helmet would be saying from my heart several things: First, no matter what had happened, God was good; his goodness was not based on my circumstances; it was not about me. Second, God was worthy to be served in the bad times as well as the good. And third, if God had called me to work in this mill, I would serve him here to the best of my ability. I took the sticker and carefully placed it on the side of my helmet, I opened the door and I took the first step, spiritually speaking, out of the pit and eventually back into God's presence.

The Meaning behind the Message

What was God up to in this story? He was trying to find out (or more correctly, he was trying help *me* find out) who he was in my life. Was God just a means to an end, or was he an end in himself? Had all the sacrifices I had made—like giving up my job, finances, a home—been for God, or were they just to get from God what I wanted? Did I love what I wanted to do for God more than I loved God? Wasn't this the central question God was posing to Abraham when he directed him to place Isaac on the alter? Sometimes you can only know the condition of your heart by losing something you desperately want.

Are not these the types of questions God is always placing before his people? Who is first in your life? Whom do you love? Whom do you serve?

A second strand imbedded in this story is that our happiness or fulfillment does not depend on our circumstances but on God himself. As long as I was dwelling solely on my trials and challenges, I could not live a victorious life. Paul Hawkins, my friend and one of my mentors in my early days in YWAM, always exhorted us: "Never judge God according to your circumstances, but always judge your circumstances according to the character of God." How true this is! Many times we live in what I call the "shy side of why." We continually ask the *why* question and never seem to get an answer. Maybe in the mill I should have been asking the *what* question. "Lord, it is what it is. What do I do with it?" As the late Keith Green used to say, "If you find yourself in the valley, farm it."

Finally, I think God was again teaching me what it means to serve. Could I stay in this mill and serve him first, and then actively seek to bless others? Or would I sit around and feel morose because others were being used by God and I wasn't? Was it still all about me, or was it about him?

Paul Revere's Horse

A scientific truth, before it is widely accepted, always has to be tested. A servant, to be genuine, always has to be tried.

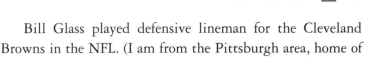

Bill Glass played defensive lineman for the Cleveland Browns in the NFL. (I am from the Pittsburgh area, home of the Steelers. There has never been any love lost between the Steelers and the Browns. Bill Glass founded Bill Glass Ministries, which later became Bill Glass Champions for Christ.)

One fall day, Glass was playing defense in a game with an NFL opponent. The ball was snapped. Glass single-handedly fought off two blockers from the opposing team. He hit the ball carrier, causing him to fumble and lose possession of the football. After two or three jarring collisions, Glass was lying on the ground. He looked up to see the football resting on the grass turf. Momentarily, a fleet little defensive back on his team came along and scooped up the ball. He trotted across the goal line, scoring a touchdown for the Browns. As Glass struggled to get to his feet, dazed and bruised by the play, he looked at the crowd in old Cleveland Stadium and saw eighty-thousand pairs of eyes trained on the defensive back. They were exuberantly applauding the defensive back's effort in scoring the touchdown. Bill thought to himself, *I guess I know what it must have been like to be Paul Revere's horse—to do most of the work and get very little of the credit.*

This, my friends, is the acid test of a servant: completing the task but allowing someone else to get the credit. Not only is this the test of being a servant, but it is also the definition of service. Service is being others-oriented, to the point that we sometimes promote or support others instead of our own purposes.

Why was I discontented in the steel mill? Because I thought I deserved a better job, a better opportunity. Other people I knew had good jobs and ministries, but I was stuck in a filthy, dark place. The test was whether I was willing to serve God and others even in this place. Or would I hold on to my wounded pride and growing doubt and serve only myself?

And why was I so disgruntled in the kitchen back in Hawaii? It was not only because of the nature of the work. It was also because I was not getting the recognition I thought I deserved. (When we think we deserve the recognition, we probably don't.) I was tried in the kitchen by not being recognized, and my reaction showed my need. Science tells us that for every action there is an equal and opposite reaction. Without question, my reaction demonstrated my lack of a servant's heart.

I started to see that the horizontal test (serving man) is directly related to the vertical test (serving God). How we respond when our service is tested on a human level reverts back to how well we have established that vertical relationship with God. When we are tempted to quit serving because we are not noticed or appreciated by people, it reveals that we have our service of man and God out of order. If our service to God is of primary importance, it does not ultimately matter what man does to us, because we are serving to please our Father in Heaven. And *God always sees.*

The Resistant Assistant

"I am tired of doing everything he doesn't want to do," the assistant pastor in Hawaii lamented to me. He was upset that he only got to preach when the pastor couldn't, and that he only got to do the jobs that the pastor could not accomplish or just didn't want to do. As I listened to his story, I thought, *Maybe this is what an assistant pastor or assistant anything does— he or she assists.*

John Dawson, president of Youth With A Mission, once said, "Sometimes wisdom is just having a keen sense of the obvious."[7] But the obvious does not seem so obvious when God is dealing with heart issues. In the kitchen, it should have been pretty clear what my role was to be. The Danish philosopher Soren Kierkegaard once said, "Life can only be understood backwards; but we must live it forward." Such is the nature of a test from God: once we come through the test we can usually see things crystal clear, but during the test we have no idea what is taking place. Being the ingenious sheep that we are, if we did have understanding, we would probably try to circumvent the process.

As I look back on my experiences in the steel mill and the kitchen, I can tell you that God was not only good but also merciful. Some things in my heart needed to die. A false god abided there: the false deity of self and self-centeredness. False gods always disappoint those who worship them. God in his mercy allowed me to encounter some hard times so I'd be spared the disillusionment that vain idols always bring to those who seek them. Once again, God had proven to be better than my best expectations and wiser than my wisest thoughts.

↻ Chapter 8

Success, God's Way

Spending the summer with a bunch of snotty-nosed kids is not my idea of success.

In 1980 I had just finished another Kona training course, and I was ready to go out and reach the world. Our team had planned a ministry trip to Australia and New Zealand, but the trip never materialized. I wondered what God had on his mind.

One day my daughter's preschool teacher, Tim, approached me. "Ken, I have an opportunity to go with a team to work in Japan. Would you fill in for me this summer?" I don't remember my initial response or even how long it took me to answer, but I can tell you that teaching in a preschool had never crossed my mind as a ministry possibility. Tim had been a faithful servant and had taught missionary kids for a long time without having the opportunity to work outside the training center in Hawaii. Mr. Tim (as the preschoolers called him) had done so much for me and all the missionary families—how could

I turn him down? So I said yes, trying to mask my lack of enthusiasm.

Tim was grateful, but there was a hitch in the process. He had not raised all the money he needed to finance his trip. He would be traveling and working with a team of sixteen missionaries, and one other team member, a young woman named Gail, also did not have her total funds. Both Tim and Gail prayed fervently for the Lord to provide, but neither one of them could raise more than half of the required fees. The deadline arrived to purchase their airline tickets. They were both still short. Tim realized that there was only one solution: they had to combine their money so one of them could go. Tim offered his funds to Gail. She received his offer with mixed feelings; her provision had come at Tim's expense.

True service always has a sacrificial aspect to it. The giving up of ourselves is always at the core of authentic service.

The story takes an interesting twist. When the final purchase of the tickets was made with the travel agency, a forgotten fact surfaced. Unbeknownst to Tim or Gail, when a group purchased fifteen tickets with this travel agency, a free ticket was awarded. Gail's ticket had been number fifteen. God had provided two tickets for the price of one! Tim and Gail left with their team for Japan to do God's work that summer.

Once again we must ask ourselves, what was going on in this story? What was the catalyst or the fuse that detonated God's blessings? It was simply people being others-oriented in their attitudes and decisions. I gave my time (which I might have wanted to use differently) and Tim gave his finances (which he might have wanted to use differently), and God gave back abundantly. You can never outgive God. True service always has a sacrificial aspect to it. Jesus came to serve, not to be served, and he did this by giving up his life for us. The giving up of ourselves is always at the core of authentic service.

So Tim went off to Japan and I became Mr. Ken, the preschool teacher. I sat around that summer with kids on my lap and all around me, reading and telling stories about Jesus. And, yes, wiping their noses. Most of the kids could not understand why my daughter, Debbie, called me Dad instead of Mr. Ken. They never could put it together.

You might be asking yourself at this point, what did you get out of it, Ken? Tim got to go to Japan. What was your reward? The reward was the joy I experienced by knowing that I, without a doubt, was doing the will of the Father that summer. The greatest benefit we get from serving is the satisfaction we receive by doing the service. There is a pre-programmed blessing in all service which is not dependent on external rewards or recognition. Something kicks in within our hearts when we simply do what Jesus would do. I can honestly say that that summer was one of the most blessed summers I spent in Hawaii.

Sometimes I wonder whether God has an eternal picture album—an album similar to ones in which you keep pictures of your family or friends when they make noteworthy accomplishments, like special performances or graduation ceremonies. I wonder what types of images God would keep in his album. What snapshots would he have of me? I would not be surprised if one of his images of success in my life was of Mr. Ken and those little ones in that humble preschool that summer.

Like a Complete Unknown

Almost everyone wants to feel that his or her life makes a difference. We yearn for significance, and to achieve a measure of success. There is nothing wrong with this, but the crux of the matter is determining the true nature of success. The Bible lays out a scenario for success that is a 180-degree turn from what is perpetuated in the culture in which we live.

For the few "somebodies" we see in life, there are a whole lot more "nobodies" quietly working behind the scenes. Most of the time the servants of Jesus Christ, who are called to be unnotables, are motivated to serve by the sheer joy of serving. Yet sometimes we feel invalidated, insignificant, like second-class citizens in the kingdom of God, like people and even God pass us by and don't even see us.

The singer-songwriter Bob Dylan, whose music has spanned five decades, expressed this feeling in the poetic lyrics of his famous song "Like a Rolling Stone":

How does it feel
How does it feel
To be without a home
Like a complete unknown
Like a rolling stone?

Dylan struck a chord with the disaffected and disconnected young people of the turbulent '60s in America. These words resonated to the center of their beings and expressed the disillusionment of their hearts. We know as Christians that we aren't supposed to feel like this, but if we are truthful, we have to acknowledge that sometimes we do.

What is the antidote to these kinds of feelings? It is to embrace God's idea about success. God is not so much concerned with the *what* of service as he is about the *why* of service. We tend to dwell on the outward or external aspect of service, but God dwells on the heart. Our victory in God's eyes is not determined by the height of our service (the level of the task as viewed by man) but by the depth of our love. The people who set up the chairs for a Sunday morning service are no less valuable than the pastor who gives the morning message. They have a different function but not a different value before God. God is not impressed with our gifts; he is the one who gave them to us! We did nothing to deserve them. He is impressed with our love and commitment to him, which motivates us to use our gifts. As a matter of fact, it may be a whole lot easier to set up chairs with a pure heart than it is to preach the morning message with one. You may be more likely to preach for the praise of man than you are to set up chairs to get people to notice you.

The Bible lays out a scenario for success that is a 180-degree turn from what is perpetuated in the culture in which we live.

Charles Swindoll, in his book *Hand Me Another Brick,* introduces a concept he calls a "willing unknown." On a trip with his family, he was driving between San Francisco and Los Angeles on the coastal highway. The surf was crashing on one side of the road, with a view of the mountains on the other side. As their car came over the crest of a hill, Swindoll reports, "We saw literally thousands of small white crosses standing at attention in perfect rank and file." Swindoll's son inquired about the meaning of this strange site. His father replied, "That's the place where they buried the men and women who died in battle. Few people remember them, son, but they are the reason we are free today." His son's eyes got big as he gazed in silence across that sacred hillside.[8] Every once in a while, when thinking about this scene, Swindoll imagined the dead to say, "Don't forget us. We are the reason you are able to drive and live and move freely in this great nation." He concluded this thought by saying, "There they lie in long silent rows, the willing unknowns."[9]

Swindoll points out that this concept of "willing unknowns" is based on two timeless truths. First, "the Lord remembers every labor done in love. With Him, nothing is ever forgotten."[10] Listen to what the Bible says in Hebrews 6:10: "For God is not unjust so as to forget your work and the love which you have shown toward His name, in having ministered and in still ministering to the saints." Every act of service we have done for him is recorded in his heavenly data bank. Yes, man forgets, but *God never does.* Second, Swindoll notes that "our rewards will be based on our faithfulness—not on public applause."[11] It is possible to get people's applause without being faithful to God. Many a ministry and individual can attest to this fact. But you can never get God's applause without being faithful to him.

The Unknown Missionary Soldier

God is pleased by those who purpose to serve others, and I think there is a particular category of Christian soldiers that catches the Lord's eye. This variety chooses to forsake familiar surroundings, friends, and family to serve God in the midst of an unfamiliar culture and location. Many such people have given up lucrative careers that provided financial security. They have relinquished their personal preferences as to how they dress and what they eat to please the One they follow. They have forgone all of this without an assurance of any measure of success. And if they do obtain some success in their work, few people will even notice. We call them missionaries.

I once heard the story of a man standing along the rail of the ship and looking at the dock below. He was returning from a short-term mission trip. He was a man who lived ahead of his time, being involved in short-term missionary ventures long before this form of missionary work became popular. Air travel had not arrived on the scene, making it necessary for him to take long ocean voyages to get to his fields of service and back. Instead of a one- or two-week mission trip as is the case today, he would venture out for three, four, or more months at a time. No organization sent him or supported him financially; he earned his own money to finance his trips.

On this trip, he was arriving back to the States at a port in New York City. As it happened, President Teddy Roosevelt and his entourage were on the same ship. Leaning over the ship's rail, watching the band play and dignitaries scurry around and the crowd eagerly waiting to welcome the president back to American soil, the missionary felt a twinge of self-pity. He thought to himself, *I go on these trips with little or no fanfare, and when I return home, not one person is here to meet me and welcome me back. I hire a taxi to get to the hotel to stay by myself, and the next morning I embark on a long train ride, again all by myself.*

Suddenly, God broke his chain of thought and spoke to his heart: "Yes, in this world people are not going to notice the things that are really important. You are going to go unnoticed even though your task is noble. But you have gotten one thing wrong. My son, you're not home yet."

When we stand before the Lord Jesus in that heavenly city to come, and we look up into his face and he says, "Well done, my good and faithful servant," it will make all our efforts worthwhile. Unknown Christian soldiers, remember the tried-and-true saying: "Only one life will soon be passed, only what is done for Christ will last." No labor of love done for God is ever in vain, for He sees and *he never, ever forgets.*

Another End

Another segment of my story comes to an end. God had taught me major lessons in more unlikely places—a kitchen, a steel mill, and a preschool. My heart's desire had always been to work in the church and to see the kingdom advance in the world. Finally, it seemed, God was going to give me the opportunity to do what I had dreamed about for so long.

Part 3

The Church and Missions

Chapter 9

Service or Disservice?

I worked for weeks preparing for the revival meetings at the church. Now I don't even want to go to tonight's meeting. What's wrong with me?

I was attending a church in Kailua-Kona, Hawaii, and had developed a friendship with the pastor of the church. The pastor and I had spoken on several occasions of the possibility of my assisting him in ministry. I submitted a request to my mission leadership that I spend half of my time working with my pastor and the church, and they concurred. It was a perfect match. The church was small, and the pastor had no other staff. I could support him in numerous areas and could learn about pastoral ministry firsthand. It was a symbiotic relationship, good for the church and good for me.

Every minute of the experience was enjoyable. My undertaking projects around the church freed the pastor to develop new areas. When he had to be away, I filled the pulpit for him. I was serving him, and he was mentoring me. Finally,

I was doing what I had always wanted to do. I was serving the church and applying the principles I had learned on the chicken farm and in the kitchen. Life was good.

One day the pastor approached me with a new church project. For some time the church had been planning a series of special revival services. A revivalist, one of the most sought-out speakers in this denomination, was scheduled to speak. I was asked to coordinate the effort. It involved organizing promotional activities, prayer support, and other activities that might be necessary to make these revival services successful. I was delighted, and with great excitement I set my hand to the task.

I organized prayer efforts targeting aspects of the upcoming meetings. I created flyers and pamphlets and recruited church members to canvas the neighborhoods to distribute literature and invite people to the meetings. I contacted the local radio station and posted flyers on telephone poles or any place I could. Promotional activities began weeks before the start of the meetings, and the closer we got to the event, the more excited I became. I sensed that God was planning on "showing up."

After much anticipation, the first day of the revival meetings was finally upon us. The revivalist had arrived. When he started to speak, I could sense that the Holy Spirit was speaking through him. God commenced to bless the meetings, and people responded by repenting and recommitting themselves the Lord. All the prayer and preparation were paying their dividends. Everything seemed great.

The meetings started on Sunday night. Monday night went well. But by Tuesday night I noticed something had changed. Prior to the start of the revival, the pastor and I had been working together. Now it was the pastor and the revivalist working in tandem, and I was sitting in the pews. I had done all the work to prepare for the meetings, and now I had been relegated to the sidelines. I was starting to feel like the odd man out. Feelings rose in my heart that were strangely familiar. God continued to move, but was I excited? Not really. Negative and critical thoughts surfaced. When the revivalist was speaking, I thought, *If I got a chance to preach in meetings like these, I could probably preach like him. He's good, but he's not that good.* What was the source of these feelings?

Then theological and hermeneutical hair-splitting dominated my thought processes. As the revivalist spoke, I would say to myself, *I don't think I agree with his interpretation of that scripture. I think he might be a bit off in the biblical basis of his message.* I developed a sudden concern for biblical "correctness." Instead of being excited about the right things God was doing, I was more concerned with whether the revivalist was doing it right. I was majoring on the minors and minoring on the majors. My attitude was slipping, and—that's right—I was losing my joy. Sound familiar?

This downward spiral continued until midweek. I arrived at the church just before lunch on Wednesday. Wednesday was the day the pastor and I met for lunch to develop our mentoring relationship. The pastor was not there when I arrived. *He must be running a little late,* I assumed. I waited patiently. Time slipped away. *He must have been unavoidably detained. He'll call me later,* I thought. I received no call from the pastor that afternoon, and that evening at the meeting he did not mention his absence. Not only had our rendezvous slipped his mind, but he didn't even realize he had forgotten. This was the straw that broke the camel's back. My deep-seated attitude problems erupted like a Hawaiian volcano. How could the pastor forget? I felt like the amazing disappearing man!

That night and throughout the next day, my offended pride rose to a new level as I started to lose my desire to be present. I had prayed and planned and worked for these meetings, and now I didn't even want to attend. It is amazing what surfaces from the human heart when life's circumstances squeeze us a bit.

How do we change our attitudes
and behaviors? Our efforts are
hopeless without God.

Being the great spiritual giant that I was, I started to realize that some things were amiss. This realization did not come in a crisis-type revelation as had happened in the past. I just started to put two and two together. The farm, the kitchen, the steel mill, and now the church had very similar story lines, with themes like wounded pride contributing to an unwillingness to serve joyfully. What did I need to do now? The same thing I did on the farm, in the kitchen, and in the mill. I had to place the responsibility directly where it belonged. The problem was not the circumstance God had allowed in my life. The villain was not my pastor. As a matter of fact, knowing the godly character of my pastor and how inclusive he had been with me up to that point, I have to conclude that God gave him a divine episode of memory loss to deal with these issues in my heart.

What was the problem? As the cartoon character Pogo once said, "We have met the enemy and he is us." I had to get real. I was willing to serve as long as I was included and treated as I thought I should be. But when not recognized or appreciated, my service took on a pretty joyless ring. I could get excited about what God was doing as long as I was central to, or at least considered part of, the process. But let those self-imposed parameters for my service be violated and my commitment to God plummeted from joyful obedience to a forced acquiescence. Coming out of my heart were what Galatians 5:19 calls "the deeds of the flesh," which include jealousy and envy, enmities and strife. Not a real pretty picture.

As was true on the farm and in the kitchen, repentance must have actions and not just words. It must be more than just a prayer. It is a 180-degree turn in our attitudes and corresponding behaviors. How do we change these things? It starts by admitting that we cannot change them. Our efforts are hopeless without God. I can't change my heart.

After establishing these facts in my mind, there were things that I could do. When jealousy or envy raised its ugly head, I could respond with gratefulness. I could thank the Lord for the privilege of supporting the pastor and the revivalist. I prayed that the Lord would bless and enrich the time my pastor and the revivalist spent together. When enmities and strife (being critical of the revivalist's theology) sought to pervade my thoughts, I responded with love and acceptance, which cover a multitude of sins. I prayed that God would bless the ministry of the revivalist, and I inclined my heart to learn from this man. I resolved to return to the meetings in my role, which was to be a prayerful, supportive attendee, and allow the pastor and the revivalist to perform their roles to lead and to preach.

I obeyed God. But to be honest, I started doing most of these things by faith and not by feeling. As I continued in prayer to bless, honor, and support those whom God had chosen to do his work, positive feelings returned. Thursday moved onto Friday, and Friday onto Saturday, and my excitement increased. My joy was not far behind.

Sunday night arrived, the final night of the revival. So much had happened in one short week. It was like God had squeezed a year's worth of dealings in my life into 168 short hours. I was sitting in the middle section of the pews toward the rear, now feeling good about what had transpired in the meetings. God had blessed people, and I had played a part in that process, and that was enough. The pastor assumed the podium and looked in my direction and asked me to stand up. Then he enumerated all the things I had done to make the meetings a success. He listed everything I had done and probably some things that I hadn't. He went on and on; it was almost embarrassing.

I sat down surprised and a little perplexed. Why had my pastor waited until this particular time to recognize my contributions? If he had done this on Monday or Tuesday, all the spiritual adjustments I went through that week could possibly have been eliminated. Later as I pondered this, the answer became evident. God is never early or late. His timing can be explained by the verse, "God is opposed to the proud, but gives grace to the humble" (James 4:6). God always acts in the most loving manner. Is it loving to affirm pride? Recognizing my accomplishments early on would have been sanctioning pride and self-centeredness—obviously not good for me or the most loving thing to do. God delayed; he waited for me to incline my heart toward humility. Then he released his extravagant affirmation at just the right time and place. God responds to us in that perfect balance between correction and approval. He never gets the two mixed up.

"Humility goes before honor" (Prov. 18:12). Prior to this experience I had a head knowledge of this principle, but it was the critical eighteen inches between my head and my heart that God was skillfully traversing. Am I saying that after this experience I was completely humble? Of course not—we're always in process. But in this one episode, God was waiting for me to incline my heart away from my purposes and toward his, which humility always leads us to do.

Often when we look back on strange or uncomfortable circumstances, they make perfect sense. Speaking about making sense of life, Steve Jobs, CEO of Apple Inc., once said, "You can't connect the dots looking forward; you can only connect them looking backward. So you have to trust that the dots will somehow connect."[12] I would add, trust God! In the end, he always connects the dots.

Chapter 10

The Law of Love

"Why don't you take these flowers and take a flying leap?" I didn't say this to the leader of our campus ministries, but the thought did cross my mind.

Do you ever find yourself in situations where, figuratively speaking, you sense that you have the cart before the horse? Where things seem to be out of order?

One of my responsibilities back in the kitchen was to maintain our cold storage area, which we called the "cool room." I maintained the inventory and kept the area clean and organized so that the food was quickly accessible at all times. Growing up, I had been taught a good work ethic, and I was determined to apply this ethic here.

Occasionally the campus ministry at our center would have a luau. "Hey, Ken, can we store the flowers for the leis in the cool room?" someone would ask. Although I almost always gave permission, I did it a bit grudgingly. My attitude was not very brotherly. I was trying to keep this area clean and organized, and people were just making my job more difficult. To be honest, I looked at helping others as something of a nuisance.

Where did this attitude originate? It came out of a heart that deemed what was necessary and unnecessary by how it affected me and my little corner of the world. Taking this to the limit gave the impression that the cool room did not exist for the training center, but that the center existed for the cool room. This was a self-aggrandizing, self-serving mentality. If we choose to walk down that road, it will lead us to the proverbial tail wagging the dog.

Another time, I was on the receiving end of this kind of attitude, and I learned how it can affect our corporate life.

Competing or Complementing?

Remember the steel mill? I had another job there. This time I worked as a hooker in the structural I-beam division. I hooked up beams for the overhead crane to ship to our customers. (I get a lot of mileage out of this job title in party games.) While completing the various aspects of my daily routine, I noticed that when I had to interface with our neighboring department, they were not very helpful. As a matter of fact, instead of working with me, they seemed to be working against me. "What is wrong with these guys?" I lamented to Jimmy, a large guy who was our hooker instructor. He responded, "Son, let me tell you how it works here." He proceeded to explain that these departments did not operate as one entity, but like US Steel and Jones and Laughlin Steel (our chief competitor). We had a monetary incentive program that rewarded increased production. When our incentive went up, theirs went down, and conversely, when theirs increased, ours took a dive. A light clicked on in my mind. This explained everything; they were just looking out for themselves.

What does this have to do with my church experience described in the previous chapter? I, too, had been looking out for number one. I hadn't been given the part in the meetings that I thought I deserved. I lost my enthusiasm and backed away from the process because it didn't benefit me. The steel-workers did not have a team mentality. Neither did I. I viewed others as having taken away what I deserved. The issue was not monetary, as was the case in the mill, but the heart issue was pretty much the same. It was selfishness.

> *We can allow ourselves to be concerned only about our ministry, to the point that we lose sight of where the church is going as a whole.*

At the risk of going from writing to meddling, let's look at this problem in relation to ministries or departments within a church. We can allow ourselves to be concerned only about our ministry, to the point that we lose sight of where the church is going as a whole. Our ministry becomes an end unto itself rather than a means to an end, which is the edification of the body. Competition arises, leading to infighting and hurt feelings and all those things that allow us to spiral downward into the abyss of failure and frustration. What is the core problem? I believe that it is too many people thinking only about themselves.

Let's broaden this web a little further. How do we interface with the other churches in the body of Christ in our community? Do we act as if there are only so many people and finances available? Are we tempted to compete instead of complement the ministries of other churches in the town or city in which we labor? If so, we have our kingdom and ministry priorities out of order and are ignoring Jesus' admonition to prefer one another. The bottom line, if this is true of us, is that our purposes take precedence over God's purposes.

There I was, working in the church, the start of a long-awaited goal. What was the first thing God did? He showed me the pride and self-centeredness of my heart. Why? Because if I was not willing to recognize and challenge these attitudes, though I had passion and zeal and maybe even a little knowledge (yet without wisdom), I would have been a hindrance rather than a help to the church's ministry.

The Bible speaks to this area of corporate and individual ministry within the church. The apostle Paul, in his instruction to the church in Ephesus, speaks of "Christ, from whom the whole body, being fitted and held together by what every joint supplies, according to the proper working of each individual part, causes the growth of the body for the building up of itself in love" (Eph. 4:15, 16). The church is under Christ and his direction. The body fits together when each of us does his or her part. We must recognize not only that we have a part, even a very special part, but also that others do too.

I had to do my part in the revival meeting, which was to organize, promote, and support. I also had to let the pastor and the revivalist do their parts, to lead and to preach. The body grows healthy when we do our part in a manner that helps the other parts, not competing or attempting to outdo them—thus fulfilling the law of love.

I have often said (jokingly) that if I ever start a ministry, I will call it Joints for Jesus, as a takeoff on Paul's admonition to let every joint fit and hold together the body of Christ. We must lovingly use our gifts and callings to serve one another. Not to get, but to give. What a different world this might be if Christendom would live and serve in this manner.

U **Chapter 11**

Taking Off Our Masks

Oh no, I am their teacher. I am not supposed to be a liar!

In all of God's dealings with me—be it on the chicken farm, in the kitchen, or in the church—the core issue that he lovingly surfaced from the depths of my heart was a little word with big ramifications. The word has an *i* in the middle. The *i* stands for when *I* was upset when *I* served in obscurity on the farm. It also represents the time when *I* was unhappy because someone else got credit for the work that *I* did in the kitchen. The *i* represents when *I* stopped serving because *I* thought *I* should have had a better role in the church revival meetings. All these *I*s are the center letter of this little word: *pride.*

Proverb 8:13 says, "Pride and arrogance and the evil way and the perverted mouth, I hate." Pride, the mentality that we can get along quite well without God, is a central concept relating to sin. Some say that pride is the root of all sin. If it is, or if it's at least one of the roots of all sin, then humility must be the way to eliminate this root. Humility is an interesting concept. We know it when we see it in a person, but it is difficult to label or define. It seems to be manifested differently in different people. How we actually receive humility is also somewhat nebulous. Richard Foster, in his book *Celebration of Discipline*, says, "Humility, as we all know, is one of those virtues that is never gained by seeking it. The more we pursue it the more distant it becomes. To think we have it is sure evidence we don't."[13] Therefore, humility must be something we do not seek or receive directly; it must be a by-product of some other pursuit.

The Way of Service

If this thing we call humility is a necessary virtue in living a victorious Christian life, how do we work it out? One way is to position ourselves to serve. This book developed out of a teaching series for Discipleship Training Schools in YWAM beginning in 1984. In these schools I taught for one week on the theme of Christian service. On one occasion a YWAM director phoned to invite me to teach a week at his center. He said to me, "I want you to do your series on humility." I paused for a few seconds and then said, "I don't have a series on humility." He replied, "Yes, you do—the one where you talk about the chicken farm and all that stuff." Call me slow or call me clueless, but I had never put the two together. Foster says, "More than any other single way, the grace of humility is worked into our lives through the Discipline of service."[14]

Can you see the wisdom of God in calling me to a farm and a kitchen? Foster says that we cannot bring about humility by ourselves, but we can do something that does—we can serve. Why is service done on the backside of nowhere, where few people take notice? It is there that God works on the desires of the flesh, our pride and arrogance. This is what surfaced in my heart when I was tested in the place of service. Foster states:

Nothing *disciplines* the inordinate desires of the flesh like service, and nothing *transforms* the desires of the flesh like serving in hiddenness. The flesh whines against service but screams against hidden service. It strains and pulls for honor and recognition. It will devise subtle, religiously acceptable means to call attention to the service rendered. . . . Every time we crucify the flesh, we crucify our pride and arrogance.[15]

Not a bad description of my reaction when I didn't receive the honor and recognition I thought I deserved!

William Law, who had a significant impact on eighteenth-century England through his book *A Serious Call to a Devout and Holy Life,* thought that every day should be a day of humility, which he believed could be developed by serving others. If we want humility, he said, we need to "be a servant of servants, and condescend to do the lowest of offices to the lowest of mankind."[16] On more than one occasion I heard Darlene Cunningham, cofounder of Youth With A Mission, say that God had called her to be a "foot washer to the foot washers." I watched her spend untold hours counseling and encouraging those whom God had called to "stay by the stuff" so that others could go out and evangelize. It has been reported that Oral Roberts's wife once said that God had called her to wash Oral Roberts's socks. Many ministry leaders would never have been able to develop their ministries without faithful spouses with servant hearts at their sides. Something happens when we purpose in our hearts to bless and champion the cause of others, which germinates the Christian virtue we call humility.

Jesus models for us the way of service and commands us to be foot washers: "If I then, the Lord and the Teacher, washed your feet, you also ought to wash one another's feet. For I gave you an example that you also should do as I did to you" (John

13:14, 15). The challenge with service is that in many cases it leads us from the spectacular to the ordinary. Foster notes that radical self-denial, such as giving up father and mother, our houses, and our lands for the sake of the gospel, has an adventurous ring to it. "But in service we must experience the many little deaths of going beyond ourselves. Service banishes us to the mundane, the ordinary, the trivial."[17] "In the realm of the spirit we soon discover that the real issues are found in the tiny, insignificant corners of our lives. Our infatuation with the 'big deal' has blinded us to this fact."[18]

> *Humility is the willingness to be known for who you really are — not more than you are, and not less than you are.*

Are we in contemporary Christian ministry so "infatuated with the big deal" that we miss the small opportunities for service that are right in front of our eyes, opportunities to reach the world one person at time? Not to mention the opportunity to let God work the grace of humility into our lives? It would behoove us to take serious the words of Bernard of Clairvaux, who once said, "Learn this lesson that, if you are to do the work of a prophet, what you need is not a scepter but a hoe."[19]

Living Authentically

In my missionary training we were taught working definitions of pride and humility. They are not perfect definitions, as none are, but for us they were a start. Humility is the willingness to be known for who you really are—not more than you are, and not less than you are. Pride, conversely, is the unwillingness to be known for who you really are. Humility emphasizes honesty, openness, and vulnerability in our lives. Pride has a tendency to cover up our flaws. Humility, in turn, desires that we be known in our weakness as well as our strengths.

Jesus had some strong words about not being authentic or real. "Woe to you, scribes and Pharisees, hypocrites! For you are like whitewashed tombs which on the outside appear beautiful, but inside they are full of dead men's bones and all uncleanness. So you, too, outwardly appear righteous to men, but inwardly are full of hypocrisy and lawlessness" (Matt. 23:27, 28). He was describing the Pharisees as if they were walking around wearing masks. The word *hypocrite* in these passages comes to us from ancient Greek plays. An actor would put on a grinning mask to recite lines of comedy. He then would go backstage to put on a sad mask and come out to recite tragic lines. The actor was called a *hupocritos,* one who wears a mask.[20] The Pharisees were putting on a front to mask who they really were—people who dwelled on external appearances rather than the spiritual condition of their hearts.

Ministry leader and teacher Malcolm Smith speaks of the results of "wearing a mask":

They (the Pharisees) assumed that to be able to grasp the truth intellectually was to be accepted by the God of the truth. Jesus rejected their assumptions. He called them hypocrites, or play actors, those who wear a mask. They masked who they were with volumes of religious expertise. But however elaborate their masks were, they were incapable of hiding lives monstrously out of step with their words. And the crowning tragedy was they believed in their masks, becoming blind to glaring inconsistencies of their attitudes and way of life.

Smith finishes by saying, "Knowing the truth is not accepting a theory, but plugging into the activity of practicing the truth."[21]

How did the Pharisees get to this place? It goes way back, to the garden. In Genesis 3 Adam and Eve are hiding from God as a result of their sin. Verses 9 and 10 record, "Then the LORD called to the man, and said to him, 'Where are you?' He said, 'I heard the sound of You in the garden, and I was afraid because I was naked; so I hid myself.'" J. Grant Howard describes how Adam is already putting on a mask.

> Forced out of hiding, Adam stands shamefacedly before his Judge and mumbles his reply. These are the first recorded words of a sinner. Note how he communicates. He mixes truth—'I was afraid'—with half-truth—'because I was naked.' The full truth was that he had disobeyed God and thus was aware of his nakedness. He did not level with God. He conceals his act of willful disobedience instead of openly and honestly confessing it. Adam can no longer function as a complete authentic person.[22]

The seed had been planted and the consequences have wreaked havoc down through human history. Charles Swindoll writes, "Since the original scene down through the centuries, the history of humanity is smeared with ugly marks of selfishness. Unwilling to be authentic, we hide, we deny, we lie, we run, we escape; anything but the whole truth!"[23]

But there is good news. God is committed to humility in our lives. Jesus says, "Beware of the leaven of the Pharisees, which is hypocrisy. But there is nothing covered up that will not be revealed, and hidden that will not be known" (Luke 12:1, 2). Most of us, if we are honest, will acknowledge that we have a fear of living openly, particularly when our openness may reveal our weaknesses or our sin. We feel that if we are open and honest, we will lose the respect and acceptance of people. It may seem logical to think this way, but it is just not true. It is a lie from the enemy. I have learned this through experience.

A Thoroughly Uncomfortable Breakfast

From 1984 to 1994 I coordinated a recruiting program for YWAM in the eastern part of the United States. On our tour we visited about thirty-five cities east of the Mississippi River to talk about world missions in general and the ministry of YWAM specifically. A local director in each city did the legwork to make the event happen. These directors were committed to world missions and saw the value of YWAM's part in that endeavor. They loved the work that we were doing. Occasionally I felt like they thought of us a little more highly than we deserved. I almost got the feeling that some of them thought that if we got cut, we wouldn't bleed. I am exaggerating, of course, but you get the picture.

One couple I worked with fell into this category. This couple came to visit my family during our time at the Rock Castle center in Powhatan, Virginia. One Sunday morning they arrived at our apartment for breakfast before church. They were in the dining area waiting while my kids and I got ready for church in the adjacent bedroom. For some reason, uncharacteristically, my youngest daughter was not being cooperative in getting ready for church. Most Sundays our family trips to church were uneventful, but on this day it was tough sledding.

The delayed obedience of my daughter coupled with the pressure to entertain our guests was getting to me. Finally, I lost it. I let my daughter have it verbally, in a very angry and unloving fashion. As soon as the words were out of my mouth, I knew I was wrong. Right away, I apologized to her and asked for her forgiveness. As most kids are, she was quick to forgive. I felt a lot better—until I remembered our guests sitting in the nearby room. Had they heard what I said? They probably had. What would they think about me now? No doubt they now believed I would bleed when cut! Thoughts like these filled my mind.

> **At that moment reality exploded in my mind. The fear of being authentic was based on an illusion.**

We finally made it out to breakfast. I sat down at the table. I looked left and then right, trying to avoid eye contact for fear of getting the look—the look that says, "How could you do something like that?" Needless to say, it was a very uncomfortable breakfast.

We finished breakfast. I returned to the bedroom and told the Lord, "This is not going to work all day. Lord, what do I do?" I felt impressed to tell the couple exactly what had happened and to ask them to pray for me. After church we went to a restaurant for lunch. We paused to pray for our food. Now was my chance. "I don't know if you heard or not," I said, "but I really lost it with my daughter this morning. I didn't handle the stress very well. Would you guys pray for me in that area?" The husband looked at me and broke out in a huge smile. At first I thought maybe he was laughing at me. Then, from his demeanor, I realized it was not that kind of smile. Grinning, he said, "That's what we like about you YWAMers. You have the *rhema*"—he liked the Greek word *rhema* (word, revelation)—"in this area of openness!"

At that moment reality exploded in my mind. The fear of being authentic was based on an illusion. The incident that I thought would bring a loss of respect, when I openly admitted it, actually heightened my guests' appreciation. I saw it afresh and anew: the enemy lies to us. He seeks to keep us in darkness. He deceives us into hiding. But God desires that we live openly and honestly before him and before people. He blesses true humility.

An Embarrassing Show-and-Tell

Living authentically has proven effective not only in missions but also in my other jobs. When I was a pubic school teacher, my supervisor arrived in my classroom to ask me a question. In my reply I told her a half-truth. A half-truth is still a whole lie. As she left my classroom, I realized what I had done—in front of my students, no less. I felt awful and asked God for forgiveness. I committed to make it right with my supervisor. A few days later I made an appointment with her. As I drove to her office that day, troubling thoughts were going through my mind like, *If you do this, you will never get a promotion.* I had to decide what was more important, my honesty or a promotion. When I arrived at my supervisor's office, I said I had not been upfront with her, and told her the truth.

After this incident I was preparing for a church discipleship class, in which I taught on subjects like being open and honest before God and man. I wondered what my class would think if they knew about my transgression. Would they be taken aback by my clay feet? I decided to tell the class. Not because I had to tell them—the sin did not involve them—but I wanted to be honest and thought maybe God could use this to teach us something.

So I laid out my offense before the class, and you know what? Not one person got up and left the class or stayed away from the class the next week because of what I had done. As a matter of fact, the students seemed to like me more after I told them the story. Do you know why? Humility always brings about unity. When we are transparent and forthcoming, it levels the playing field. It helps to dismiss the myth that, spiritually speaking, there are haves and have-nots. It says to people that we are all in this together. As the saying goes, the ground is level at the foot of the Cross.

The Bible is right again: "before honor comes humility" (Prov. 15:33).

↻ Chapter 12

Lordship

Buzz off, buddy. She burned you last night!

The story involves a young woman. The setting was a Discipleship Training School that I was leading. The young woman, whom we will call Grace, had arrived at the training center with a set of conflicting affections. Grace had been raised in a Christian home but recently had become involved with a young man who did not share her moral values. This involvement had taken its toll on her relationship and walk with God. At the urging of her mother, Grace had enrolled in our school.

As the initial weeks passed, I noticed that Grace was starting to respond to the love of God. God was very gently wooing her back to himself. One day I was teaching a session on the relinquishment of rights. The message was based on the life of Abraham and how he had to give up Isaac, through whom all God's promises to Abraham were to be fulfilled. The message of the teaching, put simply, was that there are things in our lives, some good and some bad, that if we hold on to will hinder an intimate relationship with God; they are road-blocks to our being useful to God. Normally, I would have an application or response to this teaching. I would instruct the students to take some time in prayer that afternoon, asking the Lord if there was anything that he wanted them to give to him. Was there anything in their lives that was more important to them than God? That evening we would build a bonfire where students could burn little folded sheets of paper upon which they had written whatever, if anything, God had shown them that afternoon.

On this day we were hit with a low pressure area, and the weather forecast called for twenty-four to thirty-six hours of steady rain. This sort of precluded a bonfire, but one of our staff members said, "There is no miracle in the fire. Why don't we put a candle in a bucket and do it right here in the classroom?" We decided we would give it a try. The spiritual atmosphere turned out to be just as solemn. There is always a sacred presence in meetings like these, because people bring lifelong dreams and aspirations and place them before God to take away or give back.

The students brought their notes and watched them burn slowly in the flame of the candle and turn to ash. Grace sat near the front of the classroom toward the side. As the meeting progressed, she took a picture out of her Bible. It was a picture of her boyfriend. She stared at the photo for a few moments and then put it back in the Bible. My wife, who was sitting in the back of the classroom, told me later that Grace did this at least twice. As the meeting was coming to an end, I gave one last opportunity for anyone to come forward. Grace took the picture and slowly stood up and walked up to the bucket. She carefully placed the picture in the flame. It was one of those old Polaroid pictures that seemed like it was made partly of wax. As the flame started to burn through the Polaroid, the picture bent and made a cracking sound. It was almost as if you could hear Grace's heart breaking. That night there was a change of the residents in Grace's heart—one moved out who would never totally fulfill her, and one moved in who would never, ever disappoint her.

The next morning I was walking toward the dining hall and the pay phone rang. I almost never answered the pay phone, but it rang and I was there, so I picked it up. Guess who it was? Grace's boyfriend. What do I say to him? Buzz off, she burned you last night! No, it was not my place to speak. I told someone to go get Grace. I don't know what she told the guy. I never asked her, because it was none of my business. But I do know that she finished the school, and instead of going back to her home, she worked for a couple of years as a missionary. That speaks for itself.

Anything that challenges God's supremacy and lordship is a vain idol, which God in his mercy must allow to die.

Why did God have me answer the phone that night? I think there are two reasons. First, he wanted to remind me again that words can sometimes be cheap. It is not what we say but what we do that counts. Even symbolic gestures such as burning our notes can be useless unless we are committed to follow through. The real test for Grace came not in the classroom that night—yes, maybe it started there—but when she talked with her boyfriend. That is where the rubber met the road. That is where she proved whom she really loved.

Second, God was reminding me of the importance of my relationship with him and the lordship of Christ in my life. The burning of notes was not a spiritual game we were playing but an avenue to allow God to take his rightful place in our hearts. There is room for only one *God* in our hearts. There is the capacity in our heart for many *loves,* but only after the one true God reigns supreme in it. Anything that challenges his supremacy and lordship is a vain idol, which God in his mercy must allow to die. Why? Because he knows such idols will never fulfill those who worship them.

Who Gets the Credit?

"Who gets the credit?" is a theme that continually arose in my life, whether I was on the farm, in the kitchen, or in the church. Who gets the credit for our service? The answer to this question reveals the true status of the lordship of Christ in our lives. It shows whether we truly desire to serve God, or just try to use God to serve ourselves. The Bible says that God deserves the credit for our service, for he works in us and enables our accomplishments. "I am the LORD, that is My name; I will not give My glory to another, nor My praise to graven images" (Isa. 42:8).

Ronald Reagan is given credit for instigating the events that led to the tearing down of the Berlin Wall, the symbol of Communist totalitarianism. "Mr. Reagan, you took the wall down," people were saying. What was his response? "No, I did not bring the wall down. That was part of a Divine Plan, teamwork, and God's Will."[24] This reminds me of Joseph and Pharaoh in the book of Genesis (41:15, 16). "I have heard it said about you, that when you hear a dream you can interpret it," Pharaoh inquires. Joseph responds, "It is not me; God will give Pharaoh a favorable answer." Joseph was quick not to take credit for what only God could do. William Clark, Reagan's second national security advisor, was quoted as saying, "His [Mr. Reagan's] number one maxim is that we can accomplish anything if we don't concern ourselves with who gets the credit."[25]

A Man After God's Own Heart

The church sat on beautiful Kaneohe Bay on the windward side of the island of Oahu. I was assisting another pastor with the small groups in his church. One evening, the pastor and I were attending a special meeting in a church in downtown Honolulu. A district superintendent of the Assemblies of God from the country of Sri Lanka (formerly Ceylon) was holding a series of talks. This man, Colton Wickramaratne, spoke in power and authority. It was apparent that God was blessing his ministry. As I listened to him speak and watched him minister, I thought to myself, *Why has God blessed this man?* One of the stories he told that night, which he also writes about in his book *My Adventure in Faith,* answered my question.[26]

> *Who gets the credit for our service? The answer to this question reveals the true status of the lordship of Christ in our lives.*

Colton wanted to serve God in a full-time capacity with all his heart. But to accomplish this he knew he had to attend Bible school. He twice applied to Ceylon Bible Institute and was twice turned down because of a lack of proficiency in the English language; he spoke only Sinhala. He persevered, and after a face-to-face encounter with the principal of the school, he was given a six-month probationary trial as a student. He studied English in the bathroom at night because this was the only place students were allowed to keep the lights on after 10:00 PM. After a second six-month probationary period, Colton's English was coming along and he was making great strides academically. He was looking forward to a second year of study.

Then a major roadblock arose in continuing his education. His father, who had been paying his tuition, suddenly died.

Colton now had to find another means of support. Tuition was due at the end of the month. He spent every minute of spare time crying out to God to raise up someone to support him. Three days prior the tuition due date, he requested leave to fast and pray for his provision. He returned three days later, disappointed and broken-hearted, without any change in his financial situation.

Concluding that God was calling him back to his church to be a deacon, Colton quietly acquiesced to God's will. He told the Lord that he was going to pack his bags, go back home, and get a job. He also promised to send half of his salary back to the school so someone else could study in his place.

At this point when I heard this story, the Spirit of God quickened my mind. This was the answer to my question. God found a man who didn't care *who got the credit.* Before my eyes I saw an example of a kingdom-builder who didn't covet glory for himself. If God chose to use him or someone who would go in his place, that was fine to him—so long as *God got his glory.* Colton, I realized, was truly a man after God's own heart.

But the story does not end there. That night Colton found a slip of paper with a message that the principal wanted to see him. The next morning Colton went to his office. The principal, with a smile on his face, handed him an envelope. The envelope contained US currency and a letter from a poor widow from Panama City, Florida, who explained she had been instructed in prayer to support a student at a Bible school in a place called Ceylon. She couldn't even find Ceylon on a map, but she persevered and finally found the address of the Ceylon Bible School. Her letter arrived at just the right time.

Why did the letter arrive when it did? God wanted to see if a man would choose to serve God's kingdom or his own kingdom. God is never late.

I have heard it said that when God finds someone he can trust, he always makes a way. The Bible says, "For the eyes of the LORD move to and fro throughout the earth that He may strongly support those whose heart is completely His" (2 Chron. 16:9). In Colton Wickramaratne, God had found a man he could trust, who wanted only to glorify God, and he made a way where there was no way. Nothing escapes the eyes or eludes the reach of our God.

Chapter 13

Not More, Not Less

So, you want me to ask if I can teach in this school, Lord? I don't want to be disrespectful, but students don't teach in these schools.

As my time in missions progressed, things seemed to be going well, except for one problematic area. I had always felt that God had called me to teach his Word. In the various churches I attended in my home area, I had always been involved in some sort of teaching ministry. To my puzzlement, I had not seen this gift blossom while in missions. As a matter of fact, it had remained virtually dormant. Had God withdrawn his call for me to teach?

During a staff meeting, the leader of the meeting asked a question. I thought I knew the answer. I gazed around the room wondering what the people would think if I were wrong. I kept silent. As I sat there, the Lord reminded me of a previous ministry setting. In a large prayer meeting I had felt a desire to speak out a prayer, but my eyes scanned the room and I saw what seemed to me to be long-term missionaries. I concluded that they probably could pray better than I could. I paused momentarily, the impression seemed to fade, and I remained mute. I visualized subsequent times that were pregnant with ministry opportunities for small teachings or instruction. Again, I had focused on who was in the room instead of God and concluded that others were better qualified to instruct.

Do you get the picture? I had waited to be asked to do the big teachings, missing the small opportunities God had provided. God will use us in the big things when he finds us faithful in the small things.

I was quite clever, though. I found spiritual-sounding ways of justifying my lack of response in these situations. When declining to take those small opportunities to teach, I would conclude that I did not need the limelight; I could just stay in the background and serve others with prayer. Sounds spiritual, doesn't it? But was my motive to serve? No, it was to hide. It wasn't about God's purposes; it was about mine. And this is never true service, no matter how spiritual it looks.

I had another way of soothing my conscience when I refused to allow God to speak through me. I used the Bible. I hid behind scriptures like Proverb 17:28: "Even a fool, when he keeps silent, is considered wise." *Silence is golden,* I would say to myself. For me, in these situations, I think my silence might have had more of a yellowish tint to it.

During the staff meeting, as I sat there silently, God had lovingly confronted me. I had to admit that it was not God who had prevented me from teaching; the culprit was me, and my lack of obedience in the little things. I confessed my sins of omission to God. When similar scenarios arose in the past, both verbal repentance and a practical application of my contrition were necessary. Once again, I had to put feet to my prayers. Where would these feet take me? Straight to a podium.

My First Teaching Experience

God was prodding me to approach my school leader about teaching in the school. Since I was a student, I questioned whether this was such a good idea, but God does not seem to be impressed with my arguments. The school was set up on a modular basis with visiting lecturers from around the world contributing expertise in an area of ministry. These prominent people taught for up to a week in our school. Not particularly the situation you want to cut your teeth on in your initial teaching experience. I guess it was my just reward for bypassing all the smaller opportunities God had given me.

When I had mustered enough courage, I approached our leader's ominous-looking office door. *If God is not in this, then this is the stupidest thing that I could ever have imagined,* I thought. I knocked on Bobby's door and submitted my request to teach in the school. After a momentary pause, to my surprise he said, "I think you are right. Let's do it." He told me he would get back to me about the date. I left his office feeling sort of good, until I realized that now I had to do it.

I started to pray and prepare the teaching. No word came from Bobby as to when I would teach. Several weeks passed and still nothing. Maybe he had forgotten. Was it just a test from God to see if I was willing? I kept reminding the Lord that I had been obedient and there was nothing more that I could do.

Then one day God said to me, "Go back and remind him." To say that I was hesitant would be a gross understatement. Finally, I decided that I would do it. There it was again, that office door. If you think it was difficult the first time, you should have been in my shoes this time. I entered and proceeded to profusely express how sorry I was for bothering him again. I don't remember how many times I apologized, but it was probably enough to embarrass him and me. Finally, I asked if he had forgotten about my request. "No, just waiting for the right day," he responded clearly. Timing is everything with God.

A week or so later Bobby approached me and told me that I would teach the following Wednesday. That week had an unusual schedule. There were two visiting lecturers, one teaching Monday and Tuesday and the other teaching Thursday and Friday. Who were these two speakers that I was sandwiched in between? The first was a man by the name of Dean Sherman. Being known for his keen spiritual insights and witty expressions, Dean Sherman had almost become a household name in YWAM. If the mission had a poet-laureate, he would be one of the leading candidates for the office. The other speaker was Tom Hallas. At that time, he was the YWAM leader for the nation of Australia. Tom had a heart for God and a prophetic bent to his ministry. Tom meant what he said, and said what he meant. The Word of the Lord came through this man in power and authority.

These were the two bookends that God gave me for my teaching that day. When I realized the company I would be keeping, I felt like saying, "Give me a break, God." If you struggle with this affliction of being small in your own eyes, you tend to look around and compare yourself to those around you. If you are surrounded by John Q. Average Christian, then you are pretty cool with the situation and feel free to contribute. If the people around you have name recognition or notoriety, then you make yourself less available to God. The Bible refers to this as the fear of man.

As Wednesday approached, thoughts of my inadequacy continued to mount. Watching and listening to Dean Sherman on Monday and Tuesday didn't help much, either. *Who are you to be in the same pulpit as Dean Sherman? You are going to embarrass yourself.* On and on went my thoughts. Yet deep down I realized that it was either now or never. Was I going to view myself as I thought I was, or as I thought others thought I was, or as God thought I was? I purposed in my heart that no matter how I felt, I would listen to God and follow his directive to teach that day.

> *It is my job to obey, and it is God's job to take care of the results.*

The fateful day arrived, and I gave my teaching. Was I as spiritually insightful and funny as Dean Sherman might have been? Probably not. Was I as profound and as prophetic as Tom Hallas might have sounded? Honestly, no. But you know what? I did not have to be like them, because God had not called Dean Sherman or Tom Hallas to speak that day; he had called me. That was all that mattered.

I learned a lesson that day: it is my job to obey, and it is God's job to take care of the results. God is more than able to take what we do and anoint it and bless it. That day in my teaching I spoke of being sandwiched between two great speakers, and one of the staff in the school spoke out, "You are the meat in the sandwich." God is capable of taking a little and making it much.

It was at this point that my teaching ministry really began—when I finally started walking in humility. Not trying to be more than I was, but not being less, either.

Who Has Permission?

In this book I have spoken to the servants of this world, over and over again, about their sacrificial labors. Working without recognition and giving up our rights have been constant themes. These, without a doubt, are servant-making pursuits. But we must remember that developing a servant's heart is not linked to a specific position in life but an attitude of heart. You can develop a servant's heart in a leadership position or by assuming a pulpit or by working on a chicken farm. It is not what we do but why and how we do it that counts.

Some of you reading this book may be like me. At certain junctures in your Christian walk, your working without recognition or in a supportive role may be self-inflicted rather than God-ordained. Self-inflicted in the sense that you have an unwillingness to believe and obey God as a result of an improper view of yourself, aka a poor self-image. We all realize at times that we are nothing, but God is an expert in taking nothing and making something. My younger daughter reminds me from time to time of a quote from Eleanor Roosevelt, herself confined to a wheelchair: "No one can make you feel inferior without your consent." Who determines the image you have of yourself? Is it others, is it only you, or is it God? Who has your permission?

> *God is an expert in taking nothing and making something.*

As servants of God we should never seek to be on God's lapel if he chooses to keep us in his pocket. But it is just as true that we should never seek to hide in God's pocket when he determines to put us on his lapel. Jesus instructs his followers to "let your light shine before men in such a way that they may see your good works, and glorify your Father who is in heaven" (Matt. 5:16). Pocket hiding is just as lacking in virtue as lapel seeking.

What Humility Isn't

The speaker had just finished speaking and a woman approached him. "I really enjoyed your message. You are quite a good speaker," she said. He replied, "No, I can't really speak that well." Was he being humble or just fishing for another compliment?

Sometimes to understand what something is, you have to understand what it isn't. I have spoken of a servant as one who takes second place or does some of the unwanted tasks of life. But we must understand that embracing humility does not mean we become a doormat. We defined humility as the willingness to be known for who we are. This means that we do not want to be known for more than we really are, and it means that we do not want to be known for less than we really are. Pride, the opposite of humility, is like a stick with two ends. We easily recognize the "superiority end" of boastfulness and arrogance. But it is a little more difficult for us to see the "inferiority end," which manifests itself in our having a lower view of ourselves than is true in reality. Some have labeled this as "worm pride." How can it be pride if the attitude is so self-deprecating? Because inferiority, like superiority, seeks to bring the emphasis on self. It simply uses the woe-is-me instead of the look-at-me strategy. Both are from the same source; one is just a little more disguised. The speaker in the episode at the start of this section could have passed for a humble soul, but was it an attention-getting mechanism to feel better about himself? Humility is not synonymous with a poor self-image.

How do you acquire your self-concept? There are basically three ways to view yourself:

1. Who you are (God's view).
2. Who you think you are.
3. Who you think others think you are.

Number 3 is influenced by number 2, but neither may be based on reality. How God views you is the only true source of information.

This point is illustrated in Numbers 13, when Moses sends out one man from each of the tribes of Israel to spy out the land of Canaan. The majority report is not a good one. Save Joshua and Caleb, the spies speak of the size of the people and of the land that devours its inhabitants. They conclude that they cannot take the land. At the end of the chapter the spies make a very revealing statement: "There also we saw the Nephilim (the sons of Anak are part of the Nephilim); and we became like grasshoppers in our own sight, and so we were in their sight" (v. 33). Remember, they were spies; they probably did not have a great deal of interaction with the people of the land. Where did this idea that they were like grasshoppers in the eyes of the people originate? I submit that it was spawned from a grasshopper mentality within themselves and not from the Canaanites. What we think others think about us is always conditioned by what we think about ourselves.

Small in Your Own Eyes

We find two prominent figures in the Bible, King Saul and King David, who both viewed themselves as being the least or un-esteemed. But one turns out in a figurative sense to be a grasshopper, and the other literally to be a giant slayer. What led to these two opposite outcomes?

Let's look at King Saul first. Here is a snapshot of this man Saul, the future king of Israel:

> Now there was a man of Benjamin whose name was Kish the son Abiel, the son of Zeror, the son of Becorath, the son of Aphiah, the son of a Benjamite, a mighty man of valor. He had a son whose name was Saul, a choice and handsome man, and there was not a more handsome man than he among the sons of Israel; from his shoulders and up he was taller than any of the people. (1 Sam. 9:1, 2)

Saul was tall, dark (being Middle Eastern), and handsome. He was not a grasshopper by any stretch of the imagination. But knowing the disastrous end of this man and his kingship, we must conclude that what impresses man does not always impress God, and what impresses God does not always impress man.

As we follow the story, the prophet Samuel reveals to Saul all that God has in store for him. Samuel privately anoints Saul to be king, and Saul is even permitted to prophesy and test the anointing, which he finds to be real. Yet, when it comes to the time for Samuel to publicly proclaim Saul as the king of Israel, we find Saul hiding among baggage.

> Thus Samuel brought all the tribes of Israel near, and the tribe of Benjamin was taken by lot. Then he brought the tribe of Benjamin near by its families, and the Matrite family was taken. And Saul the son of Kish was taken; but when they looked for him, he could not be found. Therefore they inquired further of the LORD, "Has the man come here yet?" So the LORD said, "Behold, he is hiding among the baggage." (1 Sam. 10:20–22)

Why was he hiding among the baggage? Was it an act of modesty expressing he was inadequate for the job? I don't think so. When God says that we can do something, it is not humility to say we can't. Timidity or possibly stupidity is a more apt description. No, Saul's gesture did not express the grace of humility, rather unbelief in the faithfulness of God.

What was the basis of the unbelief in this man's life? A rhetorical question by Samuel may give us some insight as to the answer. Samuel says to Saul, "Is it not true, though you were *little in your own eyes,* you were made the head of the tribes of Israel?" (1 Sam. 15:17, emphasis added). Was it how Saul viewed himself that contributed to his unbelief? In modern psychological jargon, it would be called a low self-image. This negative attitude toward oneself can hinder the plans and purposes of God for our lives. A poor self-image, with the associated pride and unbelief, was Saul's downfall. Our perception of ourselves is critically important, and a correct self-image comes not from how we think others see us or even our own opinion about ourselves, but through how our Father in heaven sees us.

Faith versus Unbelief

A changing of the guard was taking place. Samuel was going to anoint the next king of Israel to replace King Saul. All of Jesse's sons were decked out and waiting for their chance to interview, except one. He was quietly taking care of his father's business.

The Bible portrays King David quite differently than King Saul. In 1 Samuel, David approached the battle as Goliath held Israel hostage. "Then David left his baggage in the care of the baggage keeper, and ran to the battle line" (1 Sam. 17:22). Instead of seeing hesitation and unbelief, we observe in David a sense of adventure and faith.

Both David and Saul viewed themselves initially in the same manner. In 1 Samuel 18, when King Saul was courting David to be his son-in-law, David asked a telling question: "Is it trivial in your sight to become the king's son-in-law, since I am a poor man and lightly esteemed?" (1 Sam. 18:23). David, like Saul, was small in his own eyes. But what was different? David could flip the coin over. Humility is not constantly dwelling on our weaknesses but dwelling on God's strengths. The apostle Paul says in Philippians 4:13, "I can do all things through Him who strengthens me." David had the ability to recognize his own inadequacy without short-circuiting God's adequacy in his life.

It is all about perspective—about how we focus the camera in our lives in relation to faith and unbelief. If the camera lens is set on the unbelief setting, then the image shows us only our problems. The faith setting, though still showing in the foreground of the image the reality of our weaknesses, reveals an overshadowing background of God's all-pervasive strength and sufficiency. David was a man with his camera setting on faith.

Thus, we see the dissimilar outcomes of these two lives. Saul started out large in the eyes of man (head and shoulders taller than his peers), but ended up small in the eyes of God. Before the prophet Samuel approached the family of Jesse to anoint a new king, "The LORD said to Samuel, 'How long will you grieve over Saul, since I have rejected him from being king over Israel?'" (1 Sam. 16:1). David, on the other hand, started out small in the eyes of man (the last brother to be chosen), but became a giant slayer in the eyes of his God. "After removing Saul, [God] made David their king. He testified concerning him: 'I have found David son of Jesse a man after my own heart; he will do everything I want him to do'" (Acts 13:22 NIV).

It is all about perspective. Which way do you have your lens set?

↻ Chapter 14

To the Ends of the Earth

"You church people better get out of here. You might see some things you don't want to see."

One objective of Youth With A Mission down through the years that has never changed has been a commitment to take the gospel to the ends of the earth. Loren Cunningham, YWAM's founder, has often said, "*Go* is two-thirds of *God.*" Some in the mission have jokingly suggested that someone might write a book as a takeoff of Dave Wilkerson's book *The Cross and the Switchblade,* and call it *The Cross and the Suitcase.* Someone familiar with outreaches countered, "No, call it *The Suitcase, My Cross.*" It's possible that YWAM missionaries started the wrinkled look of the 1980s. Whatever the truth may be, YWAM has been a *going* organization, in more ways than one.

In my seventeen years with this mission, I learned many of what I call "YWAMisms." These sayings represent truths about God and us and have been used to instruct and encourage missionaries around the world. They are tools of wisdom for all who seek God and serve him, even to the ends of the earth. Let's look at a few of these and see how they rang true in real-life situations.

"Where God leads, he feeds; where he guides, he provides"

The team was from the center in Kona, and excitement was high. But they had a money problem. Collectively, they had enough for their airfare to Asia, but not enough for food, housing, and ground transportation while they evangelized. They prayed and felt that all were to go—no one should be left behind. They pooled their money and purchased their tickets, but how were they going to eat?

Juan, a young man from the island of Guam, was certain that God wanted him to go with the team to Asia. Although he had not been a part of the original team, he felt he was to attach himself to the team for this outreach. But the time for the departure of the team arrived, and they left Kona without Juan. It appeared that Juan had missed it.

The team had left Kona on an inter-island flight to Honolulu and would catch an international carrier for their trip to Asia. As they arrived at Honolulu International Airport, a curious scenario confronted them. Their flight had been over-booked, and they were bumped from their flight. The airline agent advised the team that they would be monetarily compensated for being bumped from the flight. Each team member received several hundred dollars. Guess what they used the money to provide? That's right—food, housing, and ground transportation while they evangelized in Asia.

There's more! When the team calculated how much money they had for ground fees, they realized they had a surplus. They knew the extra was for Juan. They called him and said, "Pack your bags"—I think his bags were already packed—"you're coming to Asia." Juan joined the team in Honolulu, and together they preached the gospel in Southeast Asia for the next three months. *Where God leads, he feeds; where he guides, he provides.*

In my years as a missionary, I saw story after story unfold like this one. Why? Because God is committed to reaching this world, and when he finds people simple enough to believe him and obedient enough to go, he always makes a way.

"The way up is always down"

A team was working in a refugee camp on Hong Kong Island, and the director of the United Nations camp had just given the team a job. There were 150 latrines in this camp, and 145 were not operating. The refugees from the bush, knowing little about modern sanitation, had managed through misuse to render all but five latrines nonfunctional. The job for the team: clean and make the latrines functional, and teach the refugees how to use them. Not quite what I call starting at the top.

The team consisted of middle-class young adults, ages eighteen to twenty-five, who back home would probably hang out at malls. The stench from the latrines was horrible, and the sight to the eyes was enough to sicken. But the team knew that God had called them to the camp, and this was what had been placed before them. The girls on the team wore flannel shirts with perfume-soaked sleeves. When they were just about to lose their lunches, they would bury their noses in their shirts and revive just enough to continue the task. It wasn't easy but they persevered, and one by one they cleaned and restored to functional order all 150 latrines. The team then taught the refugees to use the latrines properly, and their task was completed.

Not long afterward, the camp director approached the team leader about another job. "Will you set up a post office?" the director asked. They had been having difficulty getting mail to the refugees. So the team set up a post office and streamlined mail distribution in the entire camp.

A third opportunity arose. "Could you start a bank?" the camp director asked. Money being sent from relatives and friends was not getting to the refugees. So the team started a banking system in the camp. Now remember, none of the YWAM missionaries drew a salary. Some people jokingly used to say, "YWAM stands for Youth Without Any Money." Now the youth without any money were running a bank!

How did this team go from waste management to financial management? It started by doing something no one else was willing to do. The camp official saw the team's trustworthiness and faithfulness to the tasks (be they ever so menial) that had been placed before them. As Jesus said, "Well done, good and faithful slave. You were faithful with a few things, I will put you in charge of many things" (Matt. 25:21). This all started as the team stooped to serve in the outhouses. Promotion in God's kingdom is always based on a willingness to serve. *The way up is always down.*

"Hearing what God says . . . and doing it" (Part 1)

In the early 1990s I was leading a team traveling up the East Coast, working with churches in evangelism and promoting short-term mission opportunities. Our team did creative movement, mime, music, testimonies, and preaching—all with a focus on reaching the lost. We had a contact in Jacksonville, North Carolina, who arranged some ministry opportunities for us. One day we had an unusually full schedule. The plan this day was to visit a nursing home in the morning, put on a storefront church service in the early evening, and evangelize in the red light district later that night.

The nursing home went well. The storefront church was packed and the service was going well, but in the middle of the service the air conditioner failed. It was a sultry North Carolina evening, and after the service my team looked sapped of energy. One of the team members came up to me and said, "Are we really still going out to evangelize tonight? The team is very tired." She looked at me like I had asked her to go to Siberia. I walked away thinking, *Am I being too tough on the team? Lord, what do I do?* I had a sense deep inside me—just continue.

A few minutes later, a man from the church came up to me and said, "You don't want to go to the red light district. The mall is the happening place. There is not going to be anybody in the red light district tonight." I thought, *The mall? Lord, is this from You?* I decided to send one of our team members to the red light district to spy out the land. He returned with the report, "It's packed."

We hurriedly loaded the bus, but the team seemed to be fading. As I got on the bus, I heard one of my team members say under his breath, "Ken Barnes works his people day and night." I fired up another prayer, *Lord, are you sure you want us to do this?* I still felt it—just continue.

We arrived in the red light district, and the sidewalks were packed. Jacksonville, North Carolina, is home to one of the largest Marine Corps bases in the world. It was payday and the streets were crowded with young Marines eager to spend their money until their pockets were empty. Finding a spot to do our ministry was a problem, so I approached a policeman thinking he might assist us. He politely told us to go take a hike, adding that us "church people" should not even be down here. I shot up another prayer. Just continue.

As we walked up and down the street, it got later and later and the team was growing wearier. Finally, we found a little spot on a sidewalk and quickly started to set up. A crowd was starting to form even before we were done setting up. Our friendly officer of the law showed up and told us to move, as the crowd was swelling to the point of impeding the flow of traffic in the street. Another plea for help went up. By this time I was asking, "Lord, do you really want us to do this?" The same thought came to my mind—just continue. By this time I was tempted to say to the Lord, "Then give us a break, will yuh?"

What was going on that evening? There was a battle raging in the heavenlies over the souls of these three men.

With increasing difficulty, we continued walking the street, looking for a suitable spot. The feeling that I should "cut bait and run" was growing stronger. Suddenly, I looked across the street, and there it was. A vacant lot between a tattoo shop and another commercial establishment was sitting there waiting for us. The tattoo shop was closed, but the other store was still open. The lights from the store provided the illumination we needed to do our ministry. "Thank you, Lord." We quickly got set up and started our ministry. A crowd of young marines gathered to watch. Things were going well.

And then the lights went out. The store either closed, or they turned their outside lights off because they didn't want us there. Either way, we were in the dark. "Lord, help." My prayers were getting shorter and more desperate. In less than a minute the owner of the tattoo shop, who still happened to be in his shop, turned on his lights. He told us later that it made him mad when the store turned their lights off. God can use the owner of a tattoo shop.

We continued our presentation. About halfway through our program something changed. From the time we had arrived at the church that afternoon, it had been nothing but struggles. But in the middle of our ministry time, God broke through. I can only describe it as God invading that little piece of North Carolina real estate. The presence of the Lord permeated that alleyway, and I could sense that God was touching people's hearts. An atmosphere of struggle and trial had changed to liberty and freedom.

When we gave an invitation to accept Christ, no one came forward. But as the crowd dispersed, we noticed three young marines lingering on the perimeter of our makeshift stage area. We approached them and heard a similar story from each of them, an account about being raised in a Christian home but forsaking the faith of their fathers and living in the sinful ways of the world. We ministered to them, and they confessed their sins and recommitted themselves to the Lord. That night, three of God's prodigal sons came home. One of the young marines, after his discharge, even joined our mission.

What was going on that evening? There was a battle raging in the heavenlies over the souls of these three men. We were in pursuit of these three, who were like lost sheep of the House of Israel. When I get to heaven, I believe I may run into prayer warrior parents or grandparents who were crying out to God to bring their Marine Corps sons or grandsons back home. We had the privilege of being part of the answer to those prayers.

Well after midnight as we drove back, our bodies were weary but our spirits were soaring. We rejoiced with the angels in heaven over not one but three sinners who had repented and had come home. The next morning as I pondered the events of the night before, the Lord showed me Isaiah 11:3, "And He will delight in the fear of the LORD. And He will not judge by what His eyes see, nor make a decision by what His ears hear." The Lord was saying to me, "Listen to *me,* not what you hear or even what you see, and obey me, and see what I will do." How was the battle won? It was won by *hearing what God says, and by his grace and power doing it.*

By the way, I did give the team the next day off, just in case you think I am some type of hard guy.

"Hearing what God says . . . and doing it" (Part 2)

Now that I have told a story of how I heard what God said and did it, let me tell one where I didn't. I was serving at the Rock Castle Training Center in Powhatan, Virginia, where I led the Discipleship Training Schools and coordinated the East Coast Night of Missions tour. The tour involved visiting thirty-five cities east of the Mississippi River with a team of missionaries who shared their experiences on the mission field. We held evening meetings around a dessert format.

One year, because of logistical problems, we had to cancel part of our tour. I received a call from the local director of one of the cities that had been canceled. He told me that he had made preparations for the meeting and was eagerly looking forward to our arrival. Whether he did not get the cancellation letter, or got it and just never read it, I'm not sure. The bottom line was, we had a problem.

I explained the situation to the director. He was very disappointed. He described how he had sent out four to five hundred invitations and was expecting a huge crowd. What could I do? Since I had no team to send, I would have to recruit a makeshift team from my school staff. Since the audiovisual equipment was on the West Coast, I would have to get AV equipment from the local rental store. I told the director that I would make it happen.

I persuaded and begged and put together a team. I rented, at no little expense, the multimedia equipment for a crowd of several hundred people. Then we drove from the Richmond area to the tidewater region of Virginia for the meeting. When we arrived, there was no one to meet us. And as we started to set up, the atmosphere was strangely quiet.

About a half hour before the meeting, the director and his son arrived. His son strolled up carrying a half-eaten box of vanilla wafers and plopped it down on the dessert table. I stared at the table with one partially eaten box of wafers to feed a group of several hundred. Something did not make sense.

By the time the meeting was supposed to start, a few people had trickled into the hall. We ended up with a total of ten to twelve people. We had almost as many people on the platform as we did in the audience. The volume and intensity of the media equipment was definitely overkill. I started the meeting trying to appear excited, but nothing particularly significant happened that night.

I went to bed that night feeling just a bit discouraged! And when I woke up the next morning, I was greeted by a flat tire on our vehicle. When I found time that morning, I asked the Lord, "What is all this about?" The Lord did not take very long to answer my question. I realized I had bypassed the first and most important step: I had not asked God if we were supposed to have the meeting. With the embarrassment of the miscommunication and the excitement of possibly reaching several hundred people, I had violated a basic principle of guidance—hearing what God says *first,* and then doing it.

It took me a while to live this incident down among my staff. A week later I found a box of vanilla wafers sitting on my office desk. You live and you learn. I learned that the failure to seek God first can transform a "Night of Missions" into a "Fright of Missions." To this day I do not eat vanilla wafers!

Stoop to Greatness

The thought went through my mind, *If God had head-lines in heaven describing the most significant event in our lives, what would mine be?* I envisioned several accomplishments that God might like to highlight. I thought about all the discipleship courses I had taught in YWAM and in my church. Images crossed my mind of the people who had come to faith in Christ on the evangelistic outreaches I had directed in various countries. Memories of all the Night of Missions tours, in which I had helped recruit scores of short-term missionaries, paraded through my mind. I even directed a missionary training center in Richmond, Virginia, for a period of time. *That might make a good headline,* I thought.

As I was about to create a headline from the above mentioned accomplishments, God dropped an obscure and seemingly insignificant event into my mind. The event occurred in Virginia at Rock Castle, a beautiful and sprawling facility built by the Catholic Church. We had put in a wood burning system to help heat our water. The staff took turns rising before dawn to stoke the embers. Passing the responsibility from one person to another wasn't working well. People would forget it was their turn, and cold showers greeted our shivering staff. Not a real good way to start your morning. So I decided to take on the duty of starting the fire every morning.

I rose about 5:00 AM and made my trek to the woodburning stove and ignited the fire. With the flames crackling, I pulled a chair close to the fire and opened my Bible and proceeded to have my daily time alone with God. It didn't get any better than this: sitting by a warm fire, feasting on the Word in the presence of the King of the Universe, plus having a deep satisfaction that our staff would enjoy hot showers because I had stoked the fire. The greatest reward for service is always the privilege of doing it. True service is always God-motivated but man-oriented.

As I relived this experience in my mind, I wondered if God's headline for me might simply be "Man Stokes Fire." Every skill or attitude I needed for my other positions—recruiter, training school leader, or center director—were learned in this experience or others of the same nature. I learned my most important life lessons in situations where I served God out of a motivation of love and had the privilege of blessing those who were made in God's image.

No, there are probably no headlines in heaven. But if there are, I am certain that we are all going to be surprised at the kind of stories God considers to be newsworthy. What might yours be?

The Omega and the Alpha

We have come to the end of my saga. If you are thinking, "Now I see how Ken became a servant," you have missed the point of this book, and I have failed miserably as a writer.

Remember, we never arrive. We are always in process. The truth of the matter is, the closer you get to God, the farther you realize you have to go. As the end of this life's journey approaches, the clearer we see that we are really only starting. Therefore, the end is really the beginning—the omega is the alpha.

This has not been a story about success, at least not as the world views success. It has been more about failures and weaknesses and allowing God to turn these into his brand of victory. God desires that we live authentically and openly.

> He has shown you, O man, what is good;
> And what does the LORD require of you
> But to do justly,
> To love mercy,
> And to walk humbly with your God? (Mic. 6:8 NKJV)

Walking humbly with God means seeking to be known for who we really are, in our strengths and our weaknesses. We can only do this if we cling to God's mercy and grace. We can't do it ourselves.

In this book I have talked a lot about dying to self or relinquishing our desires to fulfill God's purposes. This is not a sad thing, because, spiritually speaking, it is only in death that we can truly experience life. It is only in surrendering to God's will that we can know true freedom. It is only in giving that we can actually receive.

This has been a story about a pretty ordinary guy with an extraordinary God. There are two messages that I hope shout from the pages of this book to the servants of this world. First, every labor of love that you do for God is never forgotten. *He never, ever, forgets!* Second, don't let yourself or anyone else demean your high calling to service. The King of Glory came to serve, and you are following in his footsteps as a descendant of the "royal line." So, my servant friends, gird up your towels and *stoop to greatness.*

↻ Notes

1. A. W. Tozer, "Renewed Day by Day," *A Treasury of Wisdom: Daily Inspiration from Favorite Christian Authors,* comp. Ken and Angela Abraham (Uhrichville, Ohio: Barbour Publishing, 1998), 233–4.

2. Richard J. Foster, *Celebration of Discipline: The Path to Spiritual Growth* (San Francisco: HarperSanFrancisco, 1998), 127.

3. Alistair Begg, "God of the Ordinary," July 1, 2001, http://www.truthforlife.org/resources/message/god-of-the-ordinary/.

4. Peter Marshall, *Mr. Jones, Meet the Master: Sermons and Prayers,* ed. Catherine Marshall (New York: Revell, 1951), 147–8. Used by permission.

5. Charles R. Swindoll, *Improving Your Serve: The Art of Unselfish Living* (New York: Bantam Books, 1986), 114.

6. Gordon MacDonald, *Rebuilding Your Broken World* (Nashville: Thomas Nelson, 2003), 86.

7. John Dawson, "Taking Your City for God," lecture, YWAM Training Center, Richmond, Virginia, June 1, 1991.

8. Charles R. Swindoll, *Hand Me Another Brick: Timeless Lessons on Leadership* (Nashville: W Publishing Group, 2006), 193–5.

9. Ibid., 195.

10. Ibid., 203.

11. Ibid., 204

12. Steve Jobs, commencement address, Stanford University, Palo Alto, California, May 2005.

13. Foster, *Celebration of Discipline,* 130.

14. Ibid.

15. Ibid.

16. William Law, *A Serious Call to a Devout and Holy Life* (Nashville: Upper Room Press, 1952), 26.

17. Foster, *Celebration of Discipline,* 126–7.

18. Ibid., 135.

19. Ibid., 126.

20. Swindoll, *Improving Your Serve: The Art of Unselfish Living,* 102–3.

21. Malcolm Smith, *Jesus and the Pharisees,* audiocassette (Unconditional Love International). Used by permission.

22. J. Grant Howard, *The Trauma of Transparency* (Portland: Multnomah Press, 1979), 30.

23. Swindoll, *Improving Your Serve: The Art of Unselfish Living,* 18.

24. Paul Kengor, *God and Ronald Reagan: A Spiritual Life* (New York: ReganBooks, 2004), 215.

25. Ibid.

26. Colton Wickramaratne, *My Adventure of Faith: How One Man Dared to Trust God for the Impossible* (Springfield, Mo.: Onward Books, 2008), 58–70. Used by permission.

☝ About the Author

Ken Barnes spent seventeen years working with Youth With A Mission. He presently resides just outside Richmond, Virginia, where he is a public school teacher. He also teaches discipleship courses at his church to prepare teams for short-term mission trips.

—